VIRGINIA TEST PREP
Reading Skills Workbook
Focus on Nonfiction
Grade 5

© 2019 by V. Hawas

All rights reserved. No part of this book may be reproduced or transmitted in any form or by any means, electronic, mechanical, photocopying, recording, or otherwise without prior written permission.

ISBN 978-1690031093

TEST MASTER PRESS

www.testmasterpress.com

Reading Skills Workbook, Focus on Nonfiction, Grade 5

CONTENTS

Introduction	4
Reading Skills Practice Sets	5
Practice Set 1: Science Article	5
Practice Set 2: Biography	15
Practice Set 3: Book Review	24
Practice Set 4: Instructional Texts	34
Practice Set 5: Speech	44
Practice Set 6: Promotional Article	54
Practice Set 7: How-To Article	64
Practice Set 8: Opinion Piece	74
Practice Set 9: Interview	84
Practice Set 10: History Article	94
Practice Set 11: Flyers	104
Practice Set 12: Advertisements	114
Practice Set 13: Science Article	124
Practice Set 14: Biography	133
Practice Set 15: How-To Article	142
Practice Set 16: Opinion Piece	152
Practice Set 17: History Article	161
Practice Set 18: Speech	171
Answer Key	180

INTRODUCTION
For Parents, Teachers, and Tutors

Virginia's English Language Arts Standards

Student learning and assessment in Virginia is based on the skills listed in the *Standards of Learning* and the *Curriculum Framework*. The reading standards describe how students will be able to read and comprehend nonfiction texts. This workbook focuses specifically on giving students experience with a wide range of nonfiction texts. It provides practice understanding, analyzing, and responding to texts and will develop all the skills that students need.

Types of Nonfiction Texts

The state standards and the state tests both focus on using a broad range of challenging nonfiction texts. Students read passages with a range of formats and purposes. The passages are complex and may include items like charts, tables, graphs, diagrams, quotations, sidebars, and photographs.

This workbook provides practice with a wide variety of passage types. It includes common passage types like articles, biographies, and opinion pieces as well as more unique types like speeches, flyers, advertisements, and interviews. Each passage also includes advanced elements, and the questions help students understand and analyze these elements. The practice sets in this book will ensure that students are able to understand and analyze all types of nonfiction texts.

Types of Reading Comprehension Questions

The state tests require students to read nonfiction passages and answer questions to show understanding of the text. The tests include a wide variety of questions, including technology-enhanced questions that use online features. Students will answer multiple choice questions, multiple-select questions where more than one answer is selected, text selection questions where words or sentences are highlighted, written answer questions, and graphic response questions where students complete a table, diagram, or web. This workbook provides practice with a wide range of question types, and each passage also ends with an essay question.

Preparing for the SOL Reading Assessments

Students will be assessed each year by taking the SOL Reading assessments. This workbook will help students master these assessments. It will ensure that students have the ability to analyze and respond to all types of nonfiction texts, while having the strong skills needed to excel on the test.

Practice Set 1

Science Article

Our Solar System

Instructions

This set has one passage for you to read. The passage is followed by questions.

Read each question carefully. For each multiple choice question, fill in the circle for the correct answer. For other types of questions, follow the instructions given. Some of the questions require a written answer. Write your answer on the lines provided.

Our Solar System

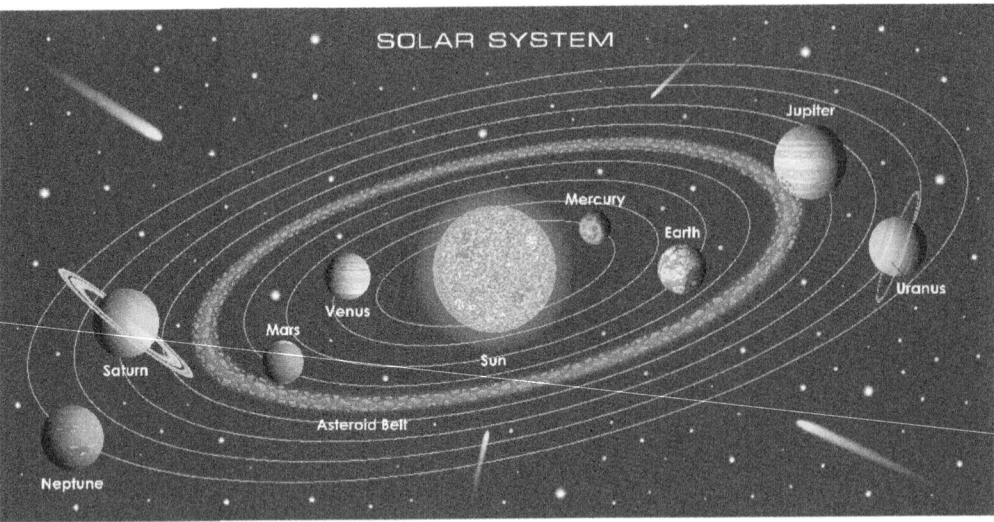

An Introduction to Our Solar System

Our Solar System is a huge place where you can find planets, dwarf planets, moons, the Sun, asteroids, comets, stars, and more! Our solar system was created 4.6 billion years ago. For many years, people believed that the Earth was the center of our universe, but it's not! The Sun is the center of our universe.

Some people believe different things about how the Solar System was created. Scientists believe that a large cloud of dust and gas began to form a spinning cloud. A small star began to form from the spinning cloud. The star got larger and larger as more dust and gas attached to it. Scientists believe that this star became the Sun. They also believe that other smaller pieces of dust and gas became the planets, smaller planets that we call dwarf planets, comets, asteroids, moons, and other stars.

How Our Solar System Works

Everything in our Solar System orbits, or goes around, the Sun. This means that the Earth and the other planets such as Mars, Jupiter, and Neptune also travel around the Sun in a path. Each planet goes around the Sun in its own path and at its own speed. The Sun is very strong and tries to pull all the planets and other objects towards it. The planets, however, are going very fast and try to pull away from the Sun. The two forces balance each other out. Each planet tries to pull away, but is also pulled toward the Sun. The end result is that each planet doesn't get either closer to or farther from the Sun. This keeps each planet in its orbit.

Our Eight Planets

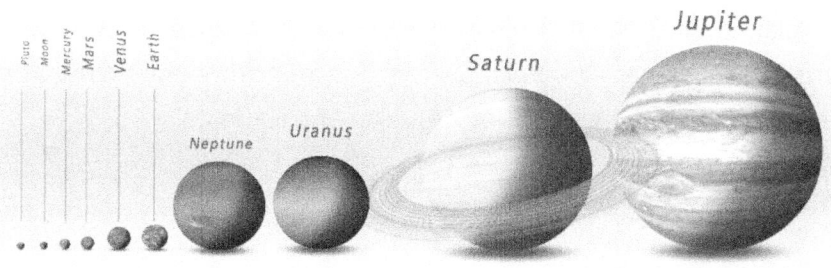

We have eight planets in our Solar System. The planet closest to the sun is Mercury, which is 36 million miles away from the Sun. This is about three times closer than Earth, which is 93 million miles from the Sun. Mercury orbits the Sun very quickly. It takes only 88 days to go around the Sun. The Earth, for example, takes 365 days to travel around the Sun. The second closest planet to the Sun is Venus. Venus's surface is made up of carbon dioxide. The carbon dioxide traps heat from the Sun, making it a very hot planet. Venus has an average temperature of about 865 degrees Fahrenheit!

Earth is the third closest planet to the Sun, and is the only planet that has life and water. After Earth is Mars, Jupiter, Saturn, Uranus, and Neptune. Mars, the fourth planet from the Sun is called the "red planet," because it is covered in a layer of red dust. Scientists have used rovers to take pictures of the landscape of Mars. We also know now that Mars has very large dust storms. They might be some of the biggest dust storms in the galaxy.

Jupiter can be recognized by its giant red oval spot in the middle of the planet. Jupiter is about 480 million miles away from the Sun and has a mass more than three hundred times bigger than the Earth. Saturn is the sixth planet from the Sun and is known for its beautiful rings. Saturn has at least three rings around the planet that can be seen only with a telescope. Saturn also has 18 or more moons.

Uranus is the seventh planet from the Sun and its center is a frozen mass of ammonia and methane. The ammonia and methane make Uranus look blue-green in color. Uranus has more moons than Saturn; it has 27 moons. The farthest planet from the sun is Neptune. Neptune is made of the gases hydrogen and helium. Jupiter, Saturn, Uranus, and Neptune are all planets that are made of gas only. The rest of the planets are made up of rock.

Dwarf Planets

Before, scientists also called Pluto a planet, but now scientists have announced that Pluto is only a dwarf planet. Pluto is now called a dwarf planet because it does not meet all the requirements to be a planet. Our Solar System has four other known dwarf planets. These dwarf planets are named Ceres, Eris, Makemake, and Haumea.

Asteroids and the Asteroid Belt

In our Solar System, we have an asteroid belt. Our asteroid belt is an area between Jupiter and Saturn where there are a lot of asteroids. Asteroids are pieces of rock and metal floating in space that never formed into a planet. We know that there are more than 7,000 asteroids. There are 26 asteroids that are more than 200 kilometers wide. Two asteroids that people have photographed and researched are Ida and Gaspra.

Moons in Our Solar System

Earth is not the only planet that has moons. In fact, only Venus and Mercury do not have moons. Saturn has many moons with interesting features. Saturn's moon Io has over 400 active volcanoes. Saturn's largest moon is Titan, which has lakes, rivers, and oceans made up of liquid methane. Europa is an icy moon of Jupiter, where scientists believe that you can find an ocean of water!

We Are Still Learning

There is a lot that scientists still can learn about our Solar System. However, people have learned a lot about our Solar System from space explorations. We learned a lot from robots and rovers that went into space, to the Moon, and even to Mars. Scientists use a lot of different tools to study the Solar System and have also studied pieces of asteroids that have fallen to the earth. People are still learning about our Solar System every day and making new discoveries.

Rovers have traveled to Mars to learn more about it. The space probe *Juno* traveled to Jupiter and orbited around it, taking photographs and collecting data.

1 Which sentence best explains why the Sun is considered the center of the Solar System?

    Ⓐ   It was created 4.6 billion years ago.

    Ⓑ   Everything orbits around it.

    Ⓒ   It is the largest object in the Solar System.

    Ⓓ   It is actually a star.

2 How is the second paragraph organized?

    Ⓐ   from most important to least important ideas

    Ⓑ   by main idea and supporting details

    Ⓒ   by comparing different events

    Ⓓ   in the order events occurred

3 Complete the table below by listing the names of the dwarf planets, moons, and asteroids mentioned in the passage.

Dwarf Planets	Moons	Asteroids
1. Pluto	1. Earth's Moon	1.
2.	2.	2.
3.	3.	
4.	4.	
5.		

4   Read this sentence form the passage.

Our Solar System was created 4.6 billion years ago.

Which word could best be used in place of *created*?

- Ⓐ   formed
- Ⓑ   organized
- Ⓒ   discovered
- Ⓓ   built

5   Which detail given about Mars is an opinion?

- Ⓐ   Mars is the fourth planet from the Sun.
- Ⓑ   Mars is covered in a layer of red dust.
- Ⓒ   Scientists have used rovers to explore the surface of Mars.
- Ⓓ   Mars may have some of the biggest dust storms in the galaxy.

6   The passage describes a physical feature that can be used to easily tell each planet apart. Complete the table by listing the main feature of Mars, Jupiter, and Saturn.

Main Physical Features of the Planets

Mars	
Jupiter	
Saturn	

7 Which detail given about the asteroid belt is best shown in the diagram at the start of the passage?

- Ⓐ its location
- Ⓑ the number of asteroids
- Ⓒ the size of the asteroids
- Ⓓ what the asteroids are made of

8 According to the passage, how are Mercury and Venus different from all the other planets in the Solar System?

- Ⓐ They are made of rock.
- Ⓑ They have no moons.
- Ⓒ They orbit the Sun.
- Ⓓ They have a surface of carbon dioxide.

9 Describe the two forces acting on each planet as it moves around the Sun. Explain how these forces keep each planet in its orbit.

_____

_____

_____

_____

10   Complete the table below with the data from the passage that shows two differences between the Earth and Mercury.

Differences between the Earth and Mercury

	Mercury	Earth
Distance from the Sun		
Time to Orbit the Sun		

11   The author describes how Venus's surface is made up of carbon dioxide. How does this feature affect the planet? Use **two** details from the passage to support your response.

_____

_____

_____

_____

_____

12   How does the section titled "Dwarf Planets" show that our understanding of the Solar System is always changing? Explain your answer.

_____

_____

_____

_____

_____

13 Read the claim below made about Saturn's moons.

   Saturn's moons are more like Earth than the planet Saturn.

   List **two** details from the passage that support the statement.

   1: _____

   _____

   2: _____

   _____

14 Look at the art at the end of the passage and read the caption. Explain how the art adds to the information in the section "We Are Still Learning."

   _____

   _____

   _____

   _____

   _____

   _____

15 Jupiter, Saturn, Uranus, and Neptune are all gas planets but they are also very different. Write an essay describing the differences between the planets. Use at least **three** details from the passage in your answer.

_____

_____

_____

_____

_____

_____

_____

_____

_____

_____

_____

_____

_____

_____

_____

_____

Practice Set 2

Biography

Louis Braille – Inventor of Braille for the Blind

> **Instructions**
>
> This set has one passage for you to read. The passage is followed by questions.
>
> Read each question carefully. For each multiple choice question, fill in the circle for the correct answer. For other types of questions, follow the instructions given. Some of the questions require a written answer. Write your answer on the lines provided.

Louis Braille – Inventor of Braille for the Blind

Louis Braille was from a small town near Paris, France. He was born on January 4, 1809. When he was three years old, he became blind. He had grabbed a sharp tool in his father's workshop and the tool slipped and hurt his eye. His eye got infected and the infection spread. He became blind in both eyes.

He still went to school, but it was hard to learn because he could not see. He had to learn by listening to what the teacher or other students told him. A few years later, Louis went to a school in Paris for blind students. Most of the teachers talked to the students. Again, Louis had to learn only by listening. He longed to read. The library had only 14 large books. The books had raised letters that you had to feel with your hands. You had to read one letter at a time instead of reading words. It took a long time to even read a page. It was hard to remember what he read.

Then a soldier named Charles Barbier visited the school. He shared a code that the soldiers used. It was called "night writing." The writing was made up of 12 raised dots that you read with your fingers. The raised dots were not letters; they were sounds. This code was used by soldiers who shared information on the battlefield without speaking. That way the enemy would not know where the soldiers were or what they were going to do next.

Barbier told the students that the code was hard to learn. But Louis easily got it. However, he also knew that he had to make it easier for others to use. He worked on the code for three years. He made a new code that used six dots instead of 12 dots. There were three dots lined up in two rows. This was called a cell. When the dots were grouped, it stood for different letters. It also stood for punctuation marks like periods, commas, and question marks. Sometimes the dots stood for a whole word. He added symbols to be used in math and in music. There were 64 different groupings. Then he made the first Braille book in 1829. (It was not called Braille until after Louis died. The code was named Braille in honor of Louis Braille.) The book talked about these groupings. It showed others how to read and write using Louis Braille's new code.

Today, many blind people from different countries use Braille. Braille helps blind people to move around safely in public spaces. The letters are written outside of doors and buildings. Braille is used on elevators and escalators so blind people know where to go.

Louis Braille died on January 6, 1852, in Paris, France. He was only forty-three years old. But he had changed the world for those who were blind. The Braille code was a wonderful gift to the world!

How to Use Braille

When people write with Braille, they use a slate or template, and a stylus. Braille can also be written with a machine. It is called a Braillewriter. The Braillewriter is like a typewriter. But unlike the typewriter which has more than 50 keys, the Braillewriter has fewer keys. It only has six keys, a spacebar, a line spacer, and a backspace. The six keys stand for the six dots of a Braille cell.

Today, there are software programs to help blind people write and edit their work. There are also electronic devices that are small enough to fit in your backpack, briefcase, or purse. These devices are used to read and write Braille.

People read books in Braille not by seeing the letters, but by feeling them. Braille signs in public places help people understand the world.

Louis Braille's Life

January 4, 1809 – Louis Braille is born in France.

1812 (age 3) – There is an accident in Louis's father's workshop. Louis loses his sight.

1819 (age 10) – Louis moves to the Royal Institute for Blind Youth in Paris to study.

1821 (age 12) – Charles Barbier shares the night writing system with students. Louis starts to make changes to Barbier's code. This leads to his own code.

1826 (age 17) – Louis graduates and becomes a teacher at the Royal Institute for Blind Youth.

1835 (age 26) – Louis sees a doctor. He is sick with a lung disease.

January 6, 1852 (age 43) – Two days after his 43rd birthday, Louis Braille dies. His code of reading and writing spreads all around the world. It is named Braille.

Today – People all around the world who are blind use Braille to communicate and understand the world. Software programs and electronic devices are used to read and write Braille.

Reading Skills Workbook, Focus on Nonfiction, Grade 5

1. Read these sentences from the passage.

    > When he was three years old, he became blind. He had grabbed a sharp tool in his father's workshop and the tool slipped and hurt his eye. His eye got infected and the infection spread. He became blind in both eyes.

    Which statement describes how the sentences are organized?

    Ⓐ The first sentence gives a fact, and the remaining sentences give opinions.

    Ⓑ The first sentence gives a summary, and the remaining sentences give additional details.

    Ⓒ The first sentence gives the cause, and the remaining sentences describe the effects.

    Ⓓ The first sentence gives a problem, and the remaining sentences describe the solution.

2. Based on the information in the second paragraph, what was the main problem with the books the library had?

    Ⓐ They were too heavy.

    Ⓑ They were boring.

    Ⓒ They took too long to read.

    Ⓓ There were not enough of them.

3. The second paragraph describes how Louis had to learn by listening. How did Louis most likely feel at this point?

    Ⓐ motivated

    Ⓑ curious

    Ⓒ determined

    Ⓓ frustrated

4   Complete the table below by ticking the features of night writing and of Braille.

	Night Writing	Braille
Uses raised dots	☐	☐
Uses 12 dots	☐	☐
Uses 6 dots	☐	☐
Is read with the hands	☐	☐
Sets of dots stand for sounds	☐	☐
Sets of dots stand for letters	☐	☐

5   When describing Barbier's code, the author states that Louis "got it." What does this mean?

Ⓐ   He understood it.

Ⓑ   He stole it.

Ⓒ   He improved it.

Ⓓ   He created it.

6   Which year in the timeline describes how Braille became popular?

☐ 1812   ☐ 1819

☐ 1821   ☐ 1826

☐ 1835   ☐ 1852

7 How is the entry in the timeline for 1812 organized?

- Ⓐ by fact and opinion
- Ⓑ by cause and effect
- Ⓒ by problem and solution
- Ⓓ by main idea and supporting detail

8 Based on the information in the passage, describe what a cell is.

_____

_____

_____

_____

9 How did meeting Charles Barbier influence Louis? In your answer, describe how meeting Barbier helped lead to the creation of Braille.

_____

_____

_____

_____

_____

_____

10 Read these sentences from the passage.

> **Today, many blind people from different countries use Braille. Braille helps blind people to move around safely in public spaces. The letters are written outside of doors and buildings. Braille is used on elevators and escalators so blind people know where to go.**

Explain how these sentences help show the importance of Louis's work.

_____

_____

_____

_____

_____

11 The author describes the Braille code as a "wonderful gift to the world." What does calling the code a "gift" suggest about how people feel about it? Explain your answer.

_____

_____

_____

_____

_____

12 Complete the table below by describing **two** ways a typewriter and a Braillewriter are similar and **two** ways they are different.

Braillewriters and Typewriters

Similarities	Differences

13 Describe **two** ways that technology has made using Braille easier.

1: _____

_____

2: _____

_____

14 Look at the photographs at the end of the passage. How do both photographs help readers understand how people read braille?

_____

_____

_____

_____

_____

15 The events in Louis's early life led him to create Braille. Describe **three** events in his life that led him to create Braille.

Practice Set 3

Book Review

Love That Dog

Instructions

This set has one passage for you to read. The passage is followed by questions.

Read each question carefully. For each multiple choice question, fill in the circle for the correct answer. For other types of questions, follow the instructions given. Some of the questions require a written answer. Write your answer on the lines provided.

Book Review: *Love That Dog*

Sharon Creech's book, *Love That Dog*, is a creative story about a boy and poetry. *Love That Dog* is written in a different way than most books. Instead of chapters, Sharon Creech organizes the book in short diary entries in the form of poems. The main character, Jack, learns how to write poetry and how to express himself. His diary entries tell a story of how he changes, but the book also explores how to understand and write poetry.

At first, Jack neither understands nor enjoys poetry. His class is given an assignment to write a poem and Jack does not think he is able to. Instead of giving up, Jack tries to write like some of the authors he has been introduced to in class. Jack likes the poem "Love That Boy" by Walter Dean Myers. The first entry he writes copies that poem, but is about a dog. This is when Jack introduces readers to his dog, Sky.

Throughout the book, Jack asks many questions about poetry. He sometimes asks why a poem was written or makes fun of the subject of a poem. For instance, Jack does not understand one poem about a red wheelbarrow. I relate to Jack in this way because understanding a poem can sometimes be challenging. I did notice that even when Jack does not understand a poem, he still imitates the style in his own poetry. Eventually, Jack mentions the importance of a blue car when he writes a poem like the red wheelbarrow one he had read in class. At this point, you know that the blue car is important but you're not sure why. The author makes you curious about it and that keeps you reading.

After a while, Jack writes a full poem about the day his dog, Sky, was hit by a blue car speeding down the road. I could tell that Jack found it difficult to write this poem because his teacher kept asking about the car and Jack did not want to explain at first. Even though this poem is very sad, I thought it was great that Jack was able to write it in the first place. Jack went from refusing to write poems and thinking that poetry was pointless to writing an important poem about a difficult time in his life.

Love That Dog will always be a favorite book of mine. I was able to relate to the main character while also learning about poetry. It even encouraged me to try writing poetry of my own! At the end of the book, Sharon Creech included the poems that Jack referenced. I really enjoyed reading these poems and finding out the kinds of thoughts Jack had on them.

I think this is an important book for students to read because it reminds us that even if something is hard at first, we can get better at it and succeed in the end. Jack found a way to write poems of his own. It was something he never thought he could do. You don't have to be afraid of new things. If you keep trying, you can find a way.

It is also clever how the author uses poetry to tell a story. I think this is a great way to introduce students to poetry. It shows how poetry can be used to express emotions. And like Jack did, readers can even take these poems and change them to tell their own stories. In this way, the book can make readers think in new creative ways. It is not just a story you read. It is a book that offers a technique you can repeat over and over again. You can keep experimenting with poems and creating new versions of your own.

I understand that this book is not an action-packed adventure, an amazing science fiction story, or a funny tale that will have readers in stitches in every chapter. I think many students choose books that seem much more exciting or entertaining. However, I hope readers will give this book a chance. It is a great read, a clever book, and one that will make readers think. I challenge all readers thinking "but it sounds so boring" to think again. Pick up the book, read the first few pages, and I bet you'll find yourself hooked.

| **The Red Wheelbarrow**
By William Carlos Williams

so much depends
upon

a red wheel
barrow

glazed with rain
water

beside the white
chickens. | **Jack's Version**
From *Love That Dog*

so much depends
upon

blue car

splattered with mud

speeding down the road |

1   Read these sentences from the passage.

> **Love That Dog is written in a different way than most books. Instead of chapters, Sharon Creech organizes the book in short diary entries in the form of poems.**

How are the two sentences related?

Ⓐ   The first sentence states a fact, while the second sentence gives an opinion.

Ⓑ   The first sentence makes a claim, and the second sentence supports the claim.

Ⓒ   The first sentence describes a cause, and the second sentence gives an effect.

Ⓓ   The first sentence gives an idea, and the second sentence gives an opposing idea.

2   Based on the first paragraph, select the **one** word that best describes *Love That Dog*.

☐   action-packed   ☐   unique

☐   charming   ☐   gripping

☐   goofy   ☐   haunting

3   Explain why you selected the word you did in Question 2. Use **two** details from the first paragraph to support your answer.

_____

_____

_____

_____

_____

4 What is the main purpose of paragraphs 2, 3, and 4?

- Ⓐ to summarize the plot of the book
- Ⓑ to state the main reasons to read the book
- Ⓒ to give background information on the book
- Ⓓ to compare the book to other books

5 Read this sentence from the passage.

> **I did notice that even when Jack does not understand a poem, he still imitates the style in his own poetry.**

What does the word *imitates* mean?

- Ⓐ analyzes
- Ⓑ copies
- Ⓒ debates
- Ⓓ mocks

6 Which sentence from paragraph 4 tells how Jack changes?

- Ⓐ *After a while, Jack writes a full poem about the day his dog, Sky, was hit by a blue car speeding down the road.*
- Ⓑ *I could tell that Jack found it difficult to write this poem because his teacher kept asking about the car and Jack did not want to explain at first.*
- Ⓒ *Even though this poem is very sad, I thought it was great that Jack was able to write it in the first place.*
- Ⓓ *Jack went from refusing to write poems and thinking that poetry was pointless to writing an important poem about a difficult time in his life.*

7 Paragraph 6 has a message about –

- Ⓐ accepting change
- Ⓑ overcoming loneliness
- Ⓒ facing challenges
- Ⓓ being a leader

8 According to the review, why does Jack start writing poetry? Why does Jack start by copying other people's poems? Explain your answer.

_____

_____

_____

_____

_____

9 Based on the information in paragraph 3, how does the author of *Love That Dog* create suspense? Use **two** details from the paragraph to support your answer.

_____

_____

_____

_____

_____

10 Describe **two** ways the book made the author of the review more interested in poetry.

1. _____

_____

2. _____

_____

11 The last paragraph includes the phrases "have readers in stitches" and "find yourself hooked." Explain the meaning of each phrase.

"have readers in stitches"

_____

_____

"find yourself hooked"

_____

_____

12 Read these sentences from the passage.

> **It is not just a story you read. It is a book that offers a technique you can repeat over and over again.**

What technique is the author referring to? Use details from the passage to support your answer.

_____

_____

_____

_____

_____

13 In the last paragraph, why does the author worry that people will not give the book a chance? Use **two** details from the paragraph to support your answer.

_____

_____

_____

_____

_____

14 What do the two poems at the end of the review show about how Jack tells his story? How do they help readers understand how the book is written? Explain your answer.

_____

_____

_____

_____

15   *Love That Dog* is often described as being unique and original. Explain what makes the book unique and original. Use at least **three** details from the passage to support your answer.

Practice Set 4

Instructional Texts

Set of Three Instructional Texts

> **Instructions**
>
> This set has several passage for you to read. Each passage is followed by questions.
>
> Read each question carefully. For each multiple choice question, fill in the circle for the correct answer. For other types of questions, follow the instructions given. Some of the questions require a written answer. Write your answer on the lines provided.

Ready to Roll

Sushi is a Japanese food that is popular worldwide. A sushi roll is made by placing ingredients inside a layer of rice, and the whole roll is wrapped in nori. Nori is a type of seaweed.

One of the best things about sushi is that you can make it any way you like. Just like when you make a sandwich, you can add whatever fillings you like to eat. In Japan, it is common to have seafood as the filling. However, you can make sushi with almost anything. Chicken, beef, cucumber, avocado, and fried egg are popular choices. You can even have fun experimenting with new combinations. (Remember that if you are going to use things like cooked chicken, grilled beef, or fried egg, cook these ingredients before you start making your sushi.)

Remember that sushi isn't that different to a sandwich! It just uses rice and seaweed as the "bread." Just like a sandwich, it's all about what fillings you choose to add!

Good presentation is important! Good sushi rolls are neat. They are wrapped tight so that everything holds together. They are all the same size and perfectly round.

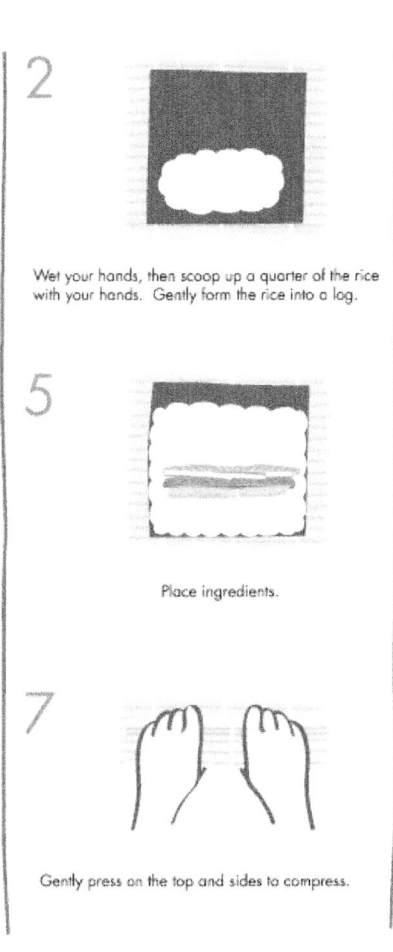

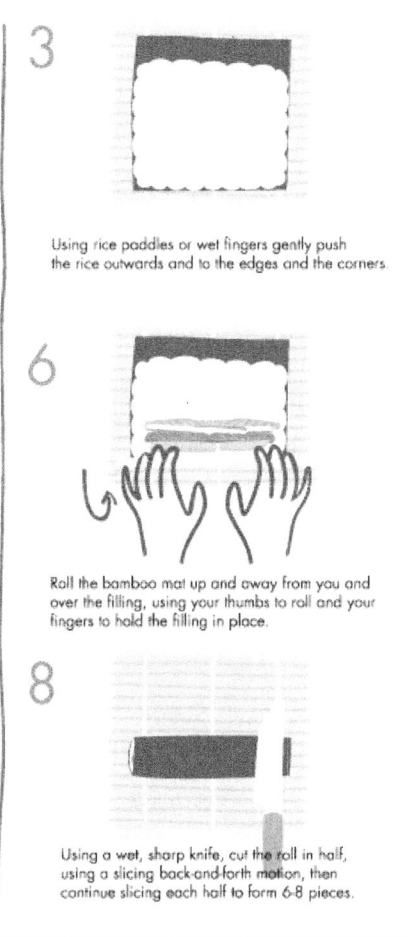

1. In the instructions, how is the sushi in Step 3 different from the sushi in Step 2?

   Ⓐ   Fillings have been added.

   Ⓑ   There has been more rice added.

   Ⓒ   The sushi roll has been cooked.

   Ⓓ   The rice has been pressed flat.

2. Which statement describes the main way the diagram in Step 5 helps readers?

   Ⓐ   It shows how many different ingredients to use.

   Ⓑ   It shows what ingredients to use.

   Ⓒ   It shows where to place the ingredients.

   Ⓓ   It shows what order to add the ingredients.

3. Which step in the instructions does the information in the second paragraph most relate to? Select the box to show your choice.

   ☐   Step 1

   ☐   Step 2

   ☐   Step 3

   ☐   Step 4

   ☐   Step 5

   ☐   Step 6

   ☐   Step 7

   ☐   Step 8

4 Describe **two** ways that a sushi roll is like a sandwich.

1: _____

_____

2: _____

_____

5 Complete the list of items needed that could be added to the instructions.

1. Bamboo mat　　　　2. _____　　　　3. Cooked rice

4. Rice paddles (optional)　　5. Filling　　　　6. _____

Explain why this list would be helpful for anyone wanting to make sushi.

_____

_____

_____

_____

6 How does the art of the rolled sushi and the caption help show the importance of being careful and gentle when completing steps 6 through 8? Explain your answer.

_____

_____

_____

_____

Get Planting!

It takes some patience to grow your own trees, but it is worth the effort. It can take months or even years for the tree to become fully grown. The good news is that it only takes a little bit of effort in the beginning. Once your tree is planted, you can let nature take care of the rest.

As long as you place the plant in the right spot, it will get enough sunlight to grow. And unless you live in a really dry climate, trees will often get enough water just from natural rainfall. After all, think of how many trees there are in a forest. Nobody runs out to water those trees every day! It is important to choose a type of tree that is suited to the climate where you live, though. This will help ensure that your tree will grow well without much effort at all from you.

And now, let's get planting.

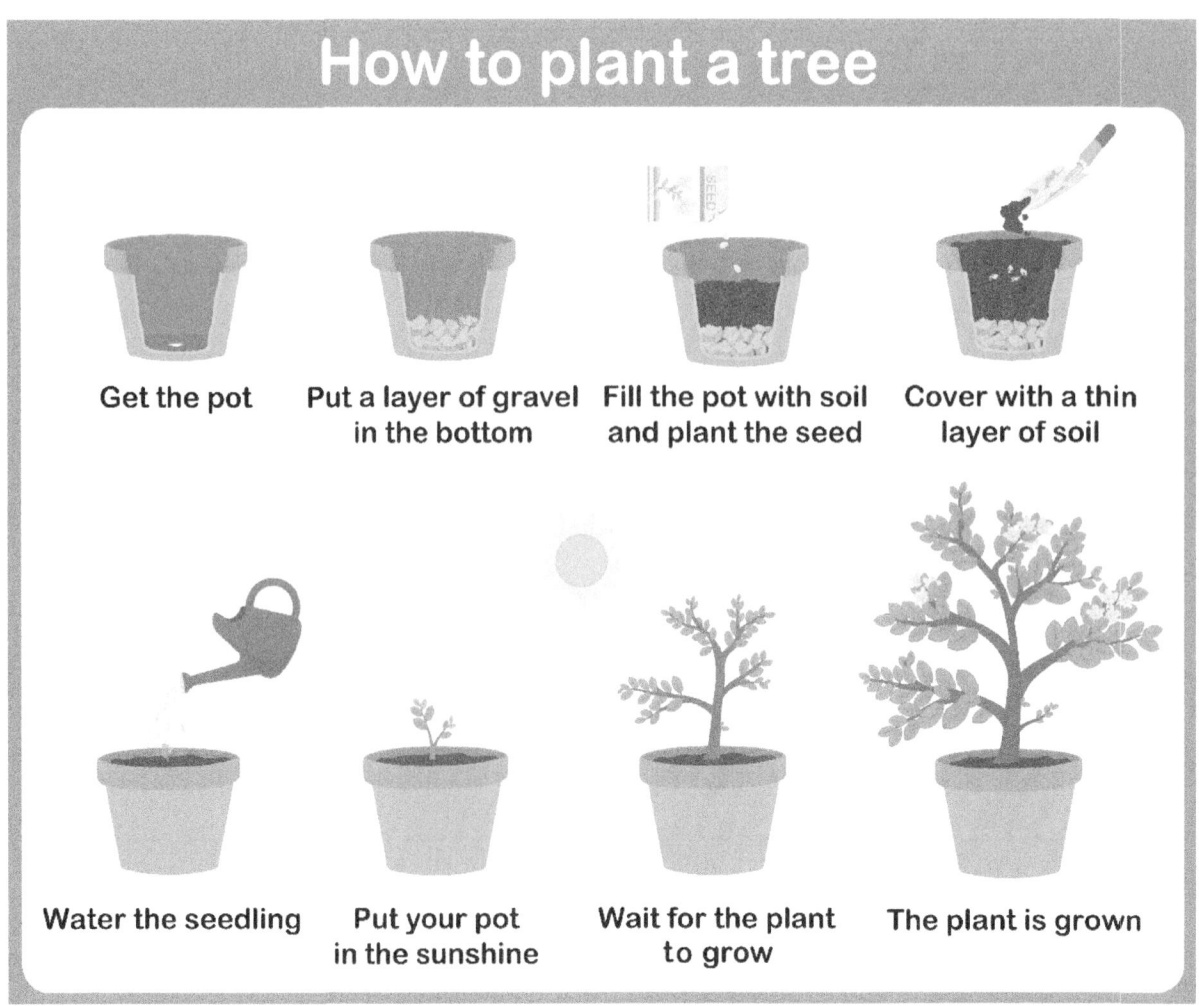

1 How is the information in the instructions organized?

  Ⓐ cause and effect

  Ⓑ problem and solution

  Ⓒ chronological order

  Ⓓ order of importance

2 Look at the illustration in Step 2 of the instructions. What additional information that is not included in the text does the illustration provide?

  Ⓐ where to place the gravel

  Ⓑ what type of gravel to use

  Ⓒ how much gravel to add

  Ⓓ why the gravel is needed

3 The author states that it takes patience to grow your own trees. Which step of the instructions would require the most patience?

  ☐ Step 1   ☐ Step 5

  ☐ Step 2   ☐ Step 6

  ☐ Step 3   ☐ Step 7

  ☐ Step 4   ☐ Step 8

4   Read these sentences from the passage.

> **After all, think of how many trees there are in a forest. Nobody runs out to water those trees every day!**

Why does the author include these sentences? In your answer, describe the main idea the author is supporting with these sentences.

_____

_____

_____

_____

_____

5   Based on the information in the passage, complete the sentences to describe how to reduce the amount of ongoing effort it takes to grow a tree.

1: Choose a tree that is _____.

2: Place the tree where it will get enough _____ and _____.

6   The passage states that growing a tree "only takes a little bit of effort in the beginning." How do the instructions support this idea? Explain your answer.

_____

_____

_____

_____

_____

Bike Hire

Samuel's town has just introduced a new bike hire program. Samuel wrote this article for the school newspaper to encourage people to use the bikes.

Did you know that our town has a new bike sharing program? The town wanted to find a way to encourage people to use their cars less and bikes more. Bikes do no use any fuel or create any pollution, so they're much better for the environment. If people use bikes more, there will also be a lot less traffic.

The program allows you to pick up a bike at many different locations. You can ride around town and then leave them at one of over 50 bike stations. Riding is a great way to see the town, and a great way to keep fit as well.

There is a cost to hire the bikes, but it's not very expensive. It's actually cheaper than a taxi and only slightly dearer than the bus. It's much better than taking a bus because you can take a bike to suit your own schedule! There's no need to be stuck waiting at a bus stop for ages. And remember that you don't have to own your own bike, so you're really saving money!

The bike program is a great thing for our town and I hope everyone supports it. Why not pick up a bike and go exploring this weekend?

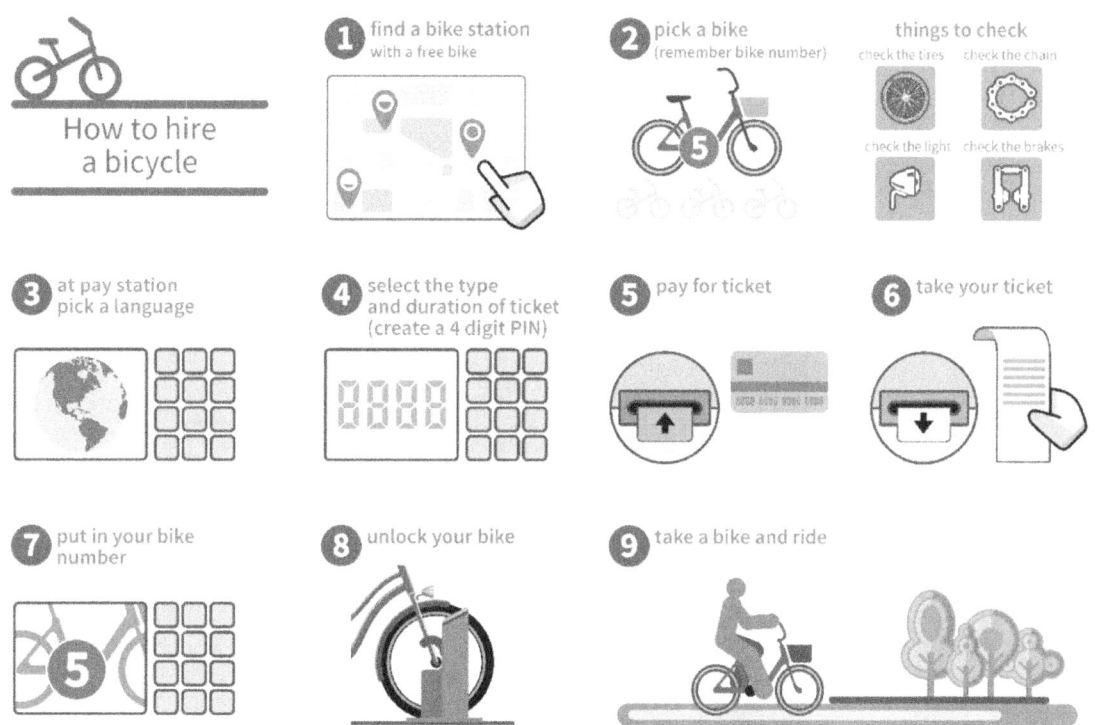

1 In Step 4 of the instructions, was does *duration* mean?

　Ⓐ　color

　Ⓑ　purpose

　Ⓒ　total cost

　Ⓓ　length of time

2 The illustration in Step 9 of the instructions mainly makes riding the bike seem –

　Ⓐ　exciting

　Ⓑ　relaxing

　Ⓒ　rushed

　Ⓓ　tiring

3 Describe **two** benefits of the bike sharing program to the town.

　1: _____

　_____

　2: _____

　_____

4. In paragraph 3, the author argues that using the bike sharing program is good value. Do you feel that the author's argument is convincing? Explain why you feel that way.

_____

_____

_____

_____

_____

5. The passage states that users can pick up a bike at many different locations. Which step of the instructions supports this idea? Explain your answer.

_____

_____

_____

_____

_____

6. The instructions list things to check on the bike. Would a user be best to do these checks at Step 2 or Step 8? Explain your answer.

_____

_____

_____

_____

_____

Practice Set 5

Speech

Make the Most of Your Time: Give it to Others!

Instructions
This set has one passage for you to read. The passage is followed by questions. Read each question carefully. For each multiple choice question, fill in the circle for the correct answer. For other types of questions, follow the instructions given. Some of the questions require a written answer. Write your answer on the lines provided.

Make the Most of Your Time: Give it to Others!
A Speech by Carly McEwen to the School Assembly

I am here today to speak to everyone in our school about something that is important to me. I am here to ask everyone here to consider making a difference to the lives of others, and yourself. I am here to talk about volunteering.

I first started volunteering when our school was doing a charity food drive. I collected and gave as many cans of food as I could. However, I could not really give a lot. I do have an allowance, but it wasn't enough to buy much. I really felt like I wanted to help everyone, but I could only do a little. I was upset, frustrated, and almost in tears about it. I complained to my mother and begged her to give more. Then my mother told me something that changed everything. She told me that I might not have money or goods, but I have plenty of time to give. She explained to me that I could do more for people by volunteering my time to good causes.

I suddenly felt like there was something I could do. The next day, we went to a local soup kitchen and I offered my help. Now I wasn't just buying a few cans for people in need. I was helping to prepare them a proper hot meal! It was hard work. I must have chopped a hundred onions that day and peeled a hundred carrots! My arms ached at the end of my shift. But I felt amazing. I helped serve too, and the people there were so grateful. The lady in charge told me how pleased the people were to see a young person helping out.

I have since been helping out at the soup kitchen every weekend. But that's not all. I also joined a local community group that does projects to clean up our town and make it look more beautiful. I have helped plant new flower gardens and have planted trees in the park. I have helped out on clean-up days where we picked up litter, removed graffiti, and repainted park benches. Everything we do is a positive experience, and I have met some great people.

And here's the best thing about my time so far with the community group. A few weeks ago, they worked on a project to clean and brighten up the river park. One of the tasks to be done was to paint colorful murals on the tired-looking brick walls of the picnic areas. I was thrilled to hear of the project and immediately offered my help. Art is one of my passions, and I knew I could help make these murals great. I actually ended up planning and designing all six murals. I drew the outlines and everyone followed my instructions to paint them. I was suddenly a leader and a project manager! The murals turned out perfect. Now every time I walk past the river park, I feel so proud of what I did.

This experience showed me that volunteering can lead to wonderful opportunities. When you volunteer, every person gets to use their unique skills to help. I would once have thought I was too young to really do much. It turned out that as an artist, I was able to really make a difference. I led a group of people who were much older than me. But nobody seemed to notice. They accepted me as the leader. They followed my plans, asked for advice, and treated me like an expert! Now, I'm not an expert. Far from it! I'm just a student with a love for art. But when you're using your skills for good, people support you and value what you can do.

I challenge all of you here to consider what you could use your unique abilities for. I never thought my artwork would be anywhere but in my art books, but now it's out in the world for everyone to see. You never know what opportunities volunteering could bring.

There are hundreds of ways you can volunteer. Choose a cause that you care about, a group that needs help, or a project that you can add your skills to. It's up to you how much time you offer. You could do just one day a week or you could get more involved. It's up to you!

I bet that once you start, you'll want to do more. I started at the soup kitchen, and I still help out there, but I wanted to do more and more. It is just such a good feeling knowing you are spending your time doing something positive and helping others. Sure, I could spend my Saturdays playing video games or browsing the mall. That can be fun, but is it really fulfilling? Does it make you feel good about yourself? Does it make you feel proud?

It's also worth thinking about how volunteering could help you in your career one day. I am learning to work with people of all backgrounds. I am learning how to communicate with people. I am learning to work as part of a team. As I've told you, I've even experienced leading a team. These are key skills that will one day help me in my career. Years from now, when I apply for college, these are going to be great things I can tell them on my application. Volunteering helps others, but it can also help you!

In closing, I want to remind you all that your age is not a problem. I started out thinking that nobody would want a kid around to help. That just wasn't true at all! Everyone was thrilled to see a young smiling face and someone with plenty of energy! I was welcomed, put to work, and made to feel as important as everyone else there.

All us of here have time we can give, and I hope you all choose to use your time wisely. Don't waste it on meaningless tasks. Of course, you can still have fun too. But spend a little of your time doing something important and helping others. I know you won't regret it. And you never know where it might lead or what you might get to do. Thank you for listening to me today and I hope to see you all out there this weekend doing good.

1   Circle the phrase from the opening paragraph that tells who the audience is.

> I am here today to speak to everyone in our school about something that is important to me. I am here to ask everyone here to consider making a difference to the lives of others, and yourself. I am here to talk about volunteering.

2   In the second paragraph, Carly describes doing the charity food drive. What problem did Carly have when doing the food drive?

   Ⓐ   She was unable to get other people interested.

   Ⓑ   She did not know who she was really helping.

   Ⓒ   She could not give as much as she wanted to.

   Ⓓ   She was not able to use her own unique talents.

3   Which sentence from paragraph 2 best helps the audience understand how Carly felt?

   Ⓐ   *I collected and gave as many cans of food as I could.*

   Ⓑ   *I do have an allowance, but it wasn't enough to buy much.*

   Ⓒ   *I was upset, frustrated, and almost in tears about it.*

   Ⓓ   *I complained to my mother and begged her to give more.*

4   Read these sentences from the speech.

   Now I wasn't just buying a few cans for people in need. I was helping to prepare them a proper hot meal!

   Which of these best describes how the information is organized?
   - Ⓐ   It compares and contrasts.
   - Ⓑ   It gives a cause and its effect.
   - Ⓒ   It states a fact and an opinion.
   - Ⓓ   It gives actions in order of importance.

5   In paragraph 4, Carly describes the work she does with the local community group. Complete the web by listing **three** more ways the group makes the town look more beautiful.

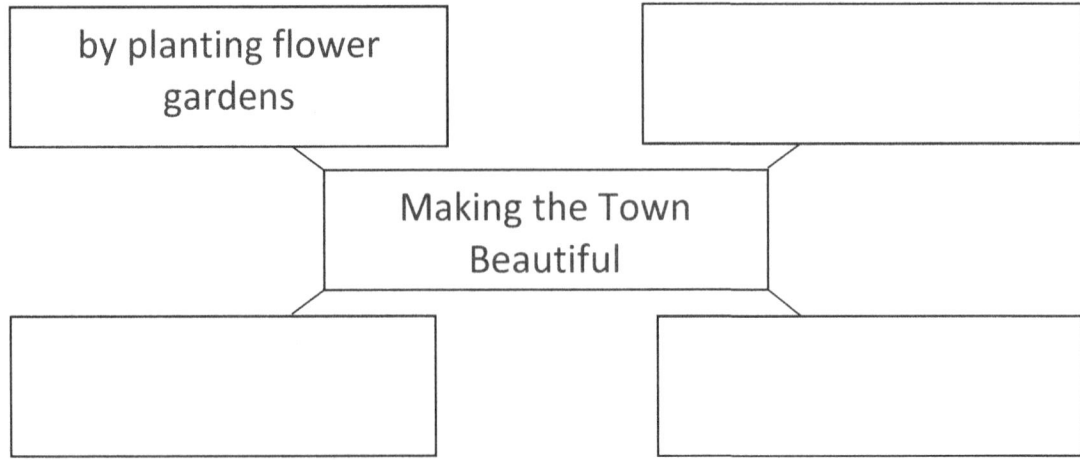

6 Which phrase from paragraph 5 tells how Carly was a leader? Select the **one** best answer.

☐ "thrilled to hear of the project"

☐ "immediately offered my help"

☐ "art is one of my passions"

☐ "make these murals great"

☐ "designing all six murals"

☐ "everyone followed my instructions"

☐ "so proud of what I did"

7 Read these sentences from the speech.

> **Now, I'm not an expert. Far from it! I'm just a student with a love for art.**

These sentences show that Carly is —

Ⓐ confident

Ⓑ determined

Ⓒ hard-working

Ⓓ humble

8   Read this sentence from paragraph 7.

> **I challenge all of you here to consider what you could use your unique abilities for.**

What does Carly tell listeners to do in paragraph 8 that has about the same meaning as the sentence above?

- Ⓐ   Choose a cause that you care about.
- Ⓑ   Choose a group that needs help.
- Ⓒ   Choose a project that you can add your skills to.
- Ⓓ   Choose how much time you are able to offer.

9   Carly says that working at the soup kitchen was hard work. Does she mind that it was hard work? Use **two** details from the passage to support your answer.

_____

_____

_____

_____

10   Why was Carly thrilled to hear of the project involving painting the murals? Use **two** details from the passage to support your answer.

11   What most surprised Carly about how the other volunteers in the community group treated her? Explain your answer.

12   Describe **two** ways that Carly believes that volunteering can help in a person's career.

   1: _____

   2: _____

13 Read these sentences from the speech.

> **Sure, I could spend my Saturdays playing video games or browsing the mall. That can be fun, but is it really fulfilling? Does it make you feel good about yourself? Does it make you feel proud?**

Why do you think Carly asks questions? What effect do you think she wants them to have on readers? Explain your answer.

_____

_____

_____

_____

14 At the end of the speech, Carly says that she hopes everyone will choose to use their time wisely. What does Carly think is a wise use of time? Use **two** details from the passage to support your answer.

_____

_____

_____

_____

15 How does Carly use her own experiences to try to make readers feel positive and excited about volunteering? Use at least **three** details from the passage in your response.

Practice Set 6

Promotional Article

Robotics Classes

Instructions

This set has one passage for you to read. The passage is followed by questions.

Read each question carefully. For each multiple choice question, fill in the circle for the correct answer. For other types of questions, follow the instructions given. Some of the questions require a written answer. Write your answer on the lines provided.

Robotics Classes

Do you want to learn about robotics in a fun, hands-on, and interactive way? Have you ever dreamed of bringing some of your drawings, designs, and creations to life? Our after-school robotics classes offer an amazing opportunity to do exactly that. For two hours a day, our team will turn your school laboratory into an authentic robotics workshop. You will have all the guidance and resources you need. Before long, you will be building and crafting robots that will wow your friends and family.

What is Special about These Classes?

Our team is passionate about allowing your creativity to run wild. So, we collaborated with many robotics experts to develop easy to use robotics kits and equipment that we can bring to your school. In the class, you will be provided with all the necessary parts, tools, and know-how to produce your own robots. Everything we provide is of top quality and easy to work with.

Using a whole range of components, you can get your robots to do a variety of different things. The best part is, you can program and control your robots from the software on laptops we provide. Of course, you will receive the needed assistance to help you along the way from our team of skilled instructors.

The classes are designed for elementary and middle school students. They are held after school so you can learn in a safe and familiar environment. Your robotics class will simply become part of your regular school day. In the class, you can work individually or with your peers – in the way that you learn best. Many schools have already signed up for our wonderful robotics classes. You could even work with other student robotics experts from other schools!

Robotics Classes Tailored to You

Many students find subjects such as science and mathematics difficult. The thought of learning about robotics can be even more daunting. Many students feel they could never learn about something so challenging. Some students, on the other hand, would love to jump right in and have a go.

Whether you're afraid to delve into robotics or are confident just to learn by trial and error, our classes are tailored to *your* needs. You can start by building the more basic sample robot designs, with assistance from the instructors. Or, if you are one of those students who is keen to jump straight in and have a go, there are a range of more challenging tasks. You could even design and build your own custom robot right from the start.

Tell Your Parents about Our Classes

Your parents are keen to make sure you learn new things and have a wide range of interests. They want you to engage with after-school activities that are fun and exciting. They also would love to be involved in your learning. Our robotics classes provide the most fun, hands-on, and inquiry-based activities that your family could wish for. Better yet, everyone can get involved. Your parents are more than welcome to join in! They can even build a few robots themselves!

Tell Your Teachers about Our Classes

Believe it or not, many teachers feel nervous about teaching difficult subjects such as robotics. Also, they often don't have the necessary equipment to teach these subjects. To order enough sets of equipment for the school would be expensive. Our robotics classes take these worries away. Teachers do not need an in-depth understanding of robotics. And we bring everything they need right to the school laboratory.

Many teachers also find it difficult to include hands-on activities in their teaching. Not only are our classes hands-on, learners are free to work at their own pace and difficulty level. They can explore their own designs and interests. The sessions are totally learner driven. That being said, your teachers are welcome to join the class at any time. Or, they can simply watch as you and your friends produce some amazing robots.

How Do I Organize Robotics Classes for My School?

First, ask your teachers about organizing robotics classes for your school. You could also talk to your parents about the classes, and they could speak to your teachers for you. Then, the teachers can go to our website and submit a request for a visit from our sales team.

We will then come to your school and demonstrate our classes during one lunch time. Teachers and parents are more than welcome to come and see how the classes work and meet our team. These "show and tell" sessions are completely free of charge. There is no obligation to sign up.

After the demonstration, our sales team will discuss the classes with your school. If the school decides to go ahead, they will then visit our website and complete an order online. After that, we will organize a date to start delivering the lessons.

If your teachers are unsure about anything, direct them to the 'For Schools' section of our website for more information. Or, they could consult with the numerous schools who have already signed up for our program.

We look forward to visiting your school soon!

1   Read this sentence from the passage.

>   **Before long, you will be building and crafting robots that will wow your friends and family.**

As it is used in the sentence, the word *wow* means to –

Ⓐ   copy

Ⓑ   help

Ⓒ   frighten

Ⓓ   impress

2   Which idea from the section titled "What is Special about These Classes?" does the art mainly relate to?

Ⓐ   Everything provided is top quality.

Ⓑ   Robots can do a variety of things.

Ⓒ   Skilled instructors will assist you.

Ⓓ   You can work with your peers.

3   Read this sentence from the passage.

>   **The thought of learning about robotics can be even more daunting.**

Which word means about the same as *daunting*?

Ⓐ   dangerous

Ⓑ   overwhelming

Ⓒ   mysterious

Ⓓ   thrilling

4 What does the author compare in the section titled "Robotics Classes Tailored to You"?

- Ⓐ how much experience students have with robotics
- Ⓑ how confident students feel about learning robotics
- Ⓒ how robotics is similar to studying science and mathematics
- Ⓓ how there are both simple and complex types of robots

5 Based on your answer to Question 4, explain why the author makes the comparison. In your answer, describe how the comparison relates to the main idea of the section.

_____

_____

_____

_____

6 Read the section titled "Tell Your Parents about Our Classes." Complete the web below by listing **four** opinions the author gives on how parents feel about their children's learning.

```
┌─────────────┐         ┌─────────────┐
│             │         │             │
└──────┬──────┘         └──────┬──────┘
       │   ┌───────────────────┐
       └───┤  Opinion on How   ├───┐
       ┌───┤   Parents Feel    ├───┘
       │   └───────────────────┘
┌──────┴──────┐         ┌──────┴──────┐
│             │         │             │
└─────────────┘         └─────────────┘
```

7 According to the section titled "Tell Your Teachers about Our Classes," how can the robotics classes save a school money?

- Ⓐ Schools do not have to employ specialist teachers.
- Ⓑ Schools do not have to purchase the expensive equipment needed.
- Ⓒ Schools do not have to train teachers in special robotics skills.
- Ⓓ Schools do not have to find ways to keep students interested.

8 Which sentence from the section titled "Tell Your Teachers about Our Classes" has about the same main idea as the section titled "Robotics Classes Tailored to You"?

- Ⓐ *Many teachers also find it difficult to include hands-on activities in their teaching.*
- Ⓑ *Not only are our classes hands-on, learners are free to work at their own pace and difficulty level.*
- Ⓒ *That being said, your teachers are welcome to join the class at any time.*
- Ⓓ *Or, they can simply watch as you and your friends produce some amazing robots.*

9 How does the author try to create enthusiasm in the first paragraph of the passage? Use **two** details from the paragraph to support your answer.

_____

_____

_____

_____

10   Based on the section titled "Tell Your Teachers about Our Classes," describe **two** ways the classes make teaching robotics easy for schools.

1: _____

_____

2: _____

_____

11   How could the robotics classes be a family activity? Use **two** details from the section titled "Tell Your Parents about Our Classes" to support your answer.

_____

_____

_____

_____

_____

12   The passage states that "many teachers feel nervous about teaching difficult subjects such as robotics." How do the robotics classes solve this problem? Explain your answer.

_____

_____

_____

_____

13 Are students able to organize robotics classes? Explain your answer.

_____

_____

_____

_____

_____

14 Complete the diagram below to show the steps involved for a school to organize starting the robotics classes.

Steps for Organizing Robotics Classes

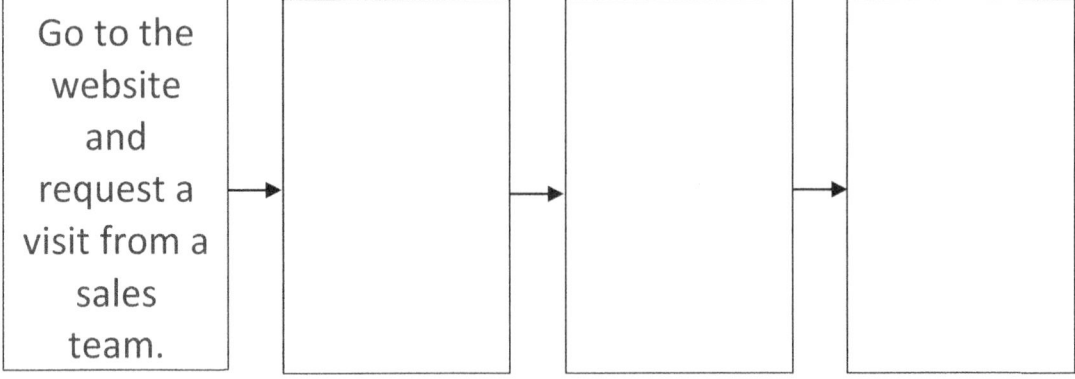

15 How do the robotics classes benefit students, parents, and schools? Use details from the passage to support your answer.

Practice Set 7

How-To Article

How to Make Magical Rice Krispie Treats

Instructions

This set has one passage for you to read. The passage is followed by questions.

Read each question carefully. For each multiple choice question, fill in the circle for the correct answer. For other types of questions, follow the instructions given. Some of the questions require a written answer. Write your answer on the lines provided.

How to Make Magical Rice Krispie Treats

When you go to a birthday party, there are always yummy treats and fun games to play. If you are lucky, there will also be a funny clown or incredible magician. But, you really want to make your next birthday party truly magical, ask your parent to help you make Magical Rice Krispie Treats. They are sure to amaze your friends!

Rice Krispie Treats are always popular at parties. But you can make yours much more special than these regular ones!

What You Will Need

To make Magical Rice Krispie Treats, you will need a few food items and a helpful adult to supervise and provide assistance.

Ingredients
- 3 tablespoons of butter
- 5 cups of mini marshmallows
- 6 cups of Rice Krispie cereal
- Food coloring of your choice

Supplies
- Large bowl
- Plastic spoon
- 1 pair of adult's rubber gloves
- 1 pair of kid's rubber gloves (must fight tightly!)
- 1 large pot
- Plastic wrap
- Large baking dish
- Cooking spray
- Butter knife
- Serving plate or platter
- Large measuring cup
- Medium-sized bowl (to hold marshmallows)
- Tablespoon

Magical Ingredients
- Gold sugar
- Rainbow sprinkles
- Chocolate chips
- Colored mini marshmallows
- Caramel drizzle
- Small bowl

It is important to keep in mind that you need to have an adult help you with each step. This can get very messy!

Preparation Instructions

To prepare, start with a clean kitchen with plenty of open counter space. Anyone helping make the Magical Rice Krispie treats should wash their hands fully with soap and warm water for at least 30 seconds. Measure out each ingredient so that it is ready to go. Once the marshmallow mixture is melted, the Rice Krispies need to be ready in the large bowl. Also, lay out all magical decorating ingredients as needed.

Instructions for Making

When you and your adult helper are ready, read through all the instructions so you know what to expect as you complete each step. Once you understand the instructions, you may begin.

1. Once hands are fully dried, put gloves on.
2. Put 6 cups of Rice Krispies into the large bowl.
3. Place 3 tablespoons of butter in a large pot and place on the stove on low or medium low heat.
4. Once butter is completely melted, add the mini marshmallows to the pot. Continuously stir until there are only a few marshmallow lumps that have not melted. This will take around 5 to 10 minutes.
5. Once there are only a few lumps that are not melted, add two drops of food dye to your marshmallow mixture. Because marshmallows are white, you should expect the final color to be pastel. Feel free to add more drops of food dye to make the color darker, but no more than six drops.
6. Once the color has blended, pour the marshmallow mixture over the Rice Krispies cereal. Stir gently until completely mixed.
7. Sprinkle a tablespoon of gold sugar and/or rainbow sprinkles over the top. Add two handfuls of chocolate chips and/or colored mini marshmallows. Stir again until mixed.

8. Lay plastic wrap in the baking dish and spray with cooking spray. Spray all gloved hands with cooking spray as well. Hands need to be greased to handle the Rice Krispie mixture. If you touch the mixture without greased hands, it will stick to you!
9. Take a small chunk of mixture from the bowl, about the size of a ping pong ball, and roll into a small ball. Place onto the greased plastic wrap. Repeat until you are completely out of mixture.
10. Sprinkle gold sugar, rainbow sprinkles, colored marshmallows, and chocolate chips lightly over treats in baking dish.
11. If you are using caramel drizzle, put 2 tablespoons into a small bowl.
12. Add 2 drops of food coloring and stir until mixed.
13. Use the spoon to drizzle colored caramel over treats.
14. Let sit for 6 hours to get firm before eating or storing.
15. Enjoy!

At Your Party

Once it is time for your party, use a gloved hand to put each treat on a fun plate. You can expect your friends to be amazed with every Rice Krispie Treat – all packed full of fun and color. Each treat will be as unique as you!

You can always try different magical decorations. Check what the baking area of your local grocery store has or you can also visit the baking area of craft stores. Sometimes you will find fun decorations you can eat, such as purple flowers, shiny pearls, or chocolate shapes. You can also use melted colored chocolate to dip your treats in, making the fun colors and decorations a surprise!

You also may find it fun to put the treat on a lollipop stick. You can place them out as a clever table decoration that you can also eat! You can also wrap them in colored plastic for gift bags or a treat that guests can take home with them!

1. What is the main purpose of the first paragraph?

    Ⓐ   to help readers imagine a situation

    Ⓑ   to give background information

    Ⓒ   to teach readers how to do something

    Ⓓ   to explain where the information comes from

2. According to the picture and caption at the start of the passage, how are Magical Rice Krispie Treats better than regular ones?

    Ⓐ   They taste better.

    Ⓑ   They are easier to share.

    Ⓒ   They are fresher.

    Ⓓ   They are more exciting.

3. Read this sentence from the passage.

    To make Magical Rice Krispie Treats, you will need a few food items and a helpful adult to supervise and provide assistance.

    Which word means about the same as *supervise*?

    Ⓐ   overuse

    Ⓑ   overcook

    Ⓒ   oversee

    Ⓓ   overtake

4 In Step 4, the instructions state to stir the mixture *continuously*. This means to stir the mixture –

- Ⓐ without stopping
- Ⓑ in one direction
- Ⓒ slowly and carefully
- Ⓓ until it has cooled

5 Select the **three** steps in which magical ingredients are added to the Rice Krispy Treats. Tick the box for each step.

☐ Step 1	☐ Step 6	☐ Step 11
☐ Step 2	☐ Step 7	☐ Step 12
☐ Step 3	☐ Step 8	☐ Step 13
☐ Step 4	☐ Step 9	☐ Step 14
☐ Step 5	☐ Step 10	☐ Step 15

6 Read the second paragraph in the section titled "At Your Party." What does this paragraph mainly suggest?

- Ⓐ Magical Rice Krispy Treats can be expensive to make.
- Ⓑ Magical Rice Krispy Treats make great gifts and party favors.
- Ⓒ You can have fun and be creative when making Magical Rice Krispy Treats.
- Ⓓ You should follow the recipe carefully to make good Magical Rice Krispy Treats.

7   Complete the web by listing **four** details the author gives in the first paragraph of things that might be part of a great party.

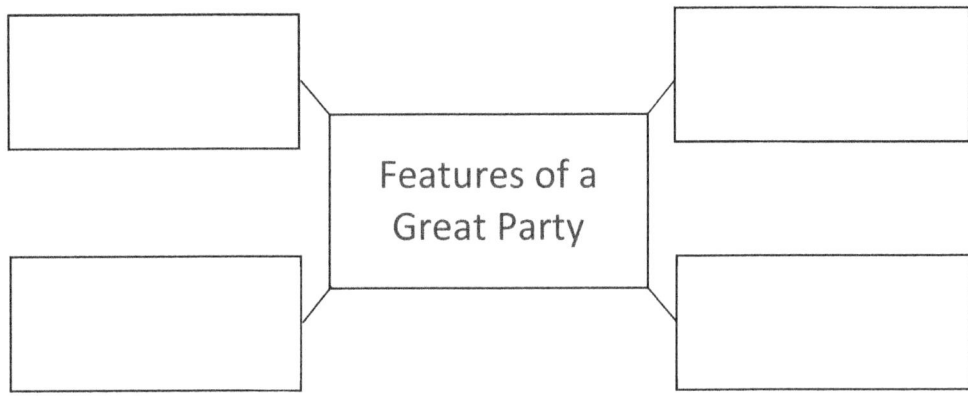

8   Describe **two** actions the author says to do in the section titled "Preparation Instructions" to be organized before starting to make the Rice Krispy Treats.

1: _____

_____

2: _____

_____

9   Why do you need to wear gloves when making Magical Rice Krispy Treats? Use **two** details from the passage to support your answer.

_____

_____

_____

_____

10. According to the passage, what is the purpose of the cooking spray? What would happen if cooking spray was not used? Explain your answer.

_____

_____

_____

_____

_____

11. Compare Step 7 of the instructions with Step 10. Describe **one** way the steps are similar and **one** way they are different.

_____

_____

_____

_____

_____

12. Identify the step that tells the size and shape to make the Magical Rice Krispy Treats. List the details below that tell the size and shape.

Size: _____

_____

Shape: _____

_____

13 The author states that each Magical Rice Krispie Treat is "packed full of fun and color." Explain how each Magical Rice Krispie Treat is colorful. Use **two** details from the passage in your answer.

_____

_____

_____

_____

_____

_____

14 Look at the photograph at the end of the passage. Which idea in the section titled "At Your Party" does the photograph relate to? Explain your answer.

_____

_____

_____

_____

_____

_____

15 Read this sentence about Magical Rice Krispie Treats.

You can make your Magical Rice Krispie Treats as unique as you like.

Describe **three** ways you could make your Magical Rice Krispie Treats unique. In your answer, describe **three** choices you could make to create unique treats.

_____

_____

_____

_____

_____

_____

_____

_____

_____

_____

_____

_____

_____

_____

_____

_____

Practice Set 8

Opinion Piece

Climate Change – What Can You Do?

Instructions

This set has one passage for you to read. The passage is followed by questions.

Read each question carefully. For each multiple choice question, fill in the circle for the correct answer. For other types of questions, follow the instructions given. Some of the questions require a written answer. Write your answer on the lines provided.

Climate Change – What Can You Do?

Dear Readers,

Many people believe that human activity is contributing to climate change. This is because cars and factories produce a large amount of greenhouse gases. These greenhouse gases go into the atmosphere. They stay in our atmosphere and trap heat from the Sun. This causes the Earth to warm up.

Lots of people are talking about climate change. This is because some feel that climate change can damage the environment and contribute to natural disasters. Many are worried that if we keep producing greenhouse gases, it will only get worse. The long-term effects could be bad for the planet and society.

Some people feel that things are out of our control. They feel like there is nothing that can be done. But I believe that there are things we can all do to help. I hope to show you how everyone can make a difference and encourage you to make some changes where possible.

We can all reduce our energy use. Small things like turning off lights and unplugging computers when they are not in use can help. Another suggestion is to wash the dishes by hand instead of using the dishwasher. Also, think about putting energy saving light globes in every room of your house.

Some appliances are needed, but you can choose to use energy efficient appliances. Many are now available and many companies work hard to make sure their appliances use as little energy as possible. When shopping for goods, remember that electrical appliances have an energy star rating. Try to seek out appliances with a high rating. This is especially important when buying big appliances. Appliances such as washing machines and fridges use up a lot of energy. Fridges are never turned off and so are always using electricity. Washing machines are often in daily use as well. It is not as important for smaller appliances like toasters and blenders that do not use up a lot of energy and are probably not used all the time.

You can save electricity by choosing appliances carefully. You can also turn them off at the wall when they are not in use.

If you need heating and cooling in your home, think about the temperature you set it to. For example, in winter, some families set the heating to a higher temperature. Instead, you could set the thermostat to a lower temperature and wear a sweater. It may even be possible to go without heating or cooling some days. Sometimes we turn on the heating or cooling when we don't really need it. Maybe you can be cool enough just by wearing light clothing. Or maybe you could be cool enough just by using a small fan instead of cooling down your whole house.

Another thing we can do in the home is wash our clothes in cold water. Many people use hot water for washing unnecessarily. Heating up water requires a lot of energy, so cold water is better. Also, hanging your clothes outside to dry is a good idea, as electric dryers also consume a lot of energy. If you are worried about the rain coming, you can always hang them inside on drying racks.

Riding your bicycle or walking to school is also a good idea. Cars produce greenhouse gas emissions, but bicycles do not and walking certainly does not. If you are worried about your safety, that's an easy problem to solve. Get other students that live nearby to walk or ride with you. It could even become a fun social activity you enjoy. Remember, too, that riding and walking will be better for your health.

We must also learn to save water. When I thought about this, I realized it will save on energy too. It takes energy to transport and process water. So, if we save water, we are saving energy. So, fix leaky taps and try to take shorter showers. Turn off the tap while you are brushing your teeth.

Recycling is also very important. If we recycle paper and cardboard by putting them in the correct trash cans, we can reduce the number of trees that need to be cut down. Trees help to reduce greenhouse gases. The more trees we have, the more greenhouse gases are removed from the atmosphere. You may even like to plant a tree. If we all planted a few trees in our lifetime, it would be good for the environment.

Reusing things is another way to help the environment. Anything we reuse won't have to be made in a factory again. If we reduce what needs to be made, we reduce the greenhouse emissions. Trash in landfills also produces greenhouse gases. So, the less waste we produce, the less greenhouse gases we produce.

You can use your creativity to find clever ways to reuse things.

Another thing to consider is what we eat. Many factories make packaging for different food products. If we eat locally grown food that isn't packaged, we can save on packaging. This will also reduce the number of factories needed for packaging. We could even have our own garden and grow our own vegetables. This doesn't require any packaging at all!

I think one of the best things you can do is tell others about climate change. Education is important. You can share some tips with your friends and family. Use the suggestions in this article to help you discuss it with them.

I have written about some simple ways that we can reduce our greenhouse gas emissions. If we implement these small changes, it will help the situation. I believe that in these small ways, we can all make a big difference. Please discuss this letter as a family and think about what you can do.

1. In the first two paragraphs, the author refers to the beliefs and opinions of "many people" and "some people." The author wants to change this information to give the opinions of a group of people that would help readers trust the information given about climate change. Which group of people would the author be best to use?

   Ⓐ farmers

   Ⓑ scientists

   Ⓒ students

   Ⓓ teachers

2. What is the main purpose of the first two paragraphs?

   Ⓐ to describe what people can do to reduce climate change

   Ⓑ to emphasize that people need to change their behavior

   Ⓒ to give background information on climate change

   Ⓓ to present facts on the history of climate change

3. How is the third paragraph different from the first two paragraphs?

   Ⓐ It shows that climate change is a major problem.

   Ⓑ It describes why climate change is occurring.

   Ⓒ It explains the impact of climate change.

   Ⓓ It focuses on what can be done about climate change.

4. According to the third paragraph, how do many people feel about climate change?

   Ⓐ angry

   Ⓑ confused

   Ⓒ frightened

   Ⓓ powerless

5. Use the information in paragraph 4 to complete the web below with **four** things that people can do to reduce energy use around the house.

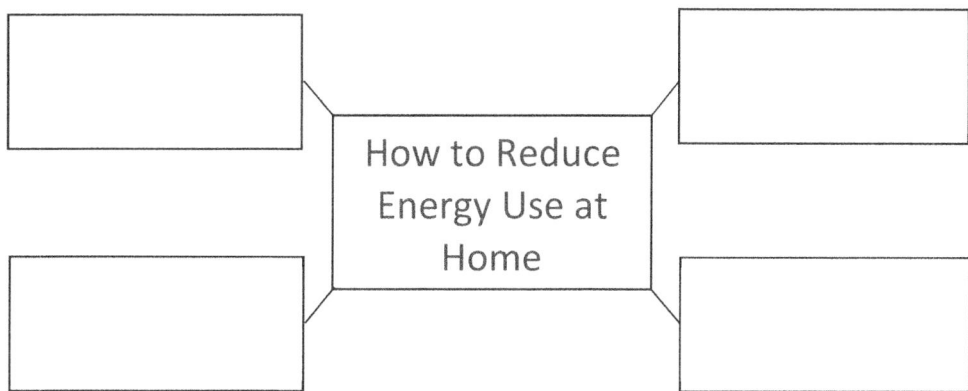

6. Which sentence from paragraph 8 states the benefit of walking or riding that relates to the main idea of the passage? Select the **one** best answer.

   ☐ Riding your bicycle or walking to school is also a good idea.

   ☐ Cars produce greenhouse gas emissions, but bicycles do not and walking certainly does not.

   ☐ If you are worried about your safety, that's an easy problem to solve.

   ☐ Get other students that live nearby to walk or ride with you.

   ☐ It could even become a fun social activity you enjoy.

   ☐ Remember, too, that riding and walking will be better for your health.

7 Which sentence from paragraph 9 describes a cause and effect?

- Ⓐ *We must also learn to save water.*
- Ⓑ *It takes energy to transport and process water.*
- Ⓒ *So, if we save water, we are saving energy.*
- Ⓓ *So, fix leaky taps and try to take shorter showers.*

8 Read this sentence from the passage.

If we implement these small changes, it will help the situation.

What does the word *implement* mean?

- Ⓐ to talk about or discuss something
- Ⓑ to put something into action
- Ⓒ to add to or increase something
- Ⓓ to care about something

9 The author states that choosing energy efficient appliances is "especially important when buying big appliances." Why would choosing an energy efficient fridge be especially important? Use **two** details from the passage to support your answer.

_____
_____
_____
_____
_____

10 Paragraph 6 describes heating and cooling. How does the paragraph suggest that people need to find a balance between being comfortable and doing the right thing for the environment? Explain your answer.

_____

_____

_____

_____

_____

11 Describe **two** ways that people can reduce energy use when doing laundry.

1: _____

_____

2: _____

_____

12 According to the author, how does recycling paper and cardboard help with climate change? Use **two** details from the passage in your answer.

_____

_____

_____

_____

_____

13 Look at the photograph of the tires on the second page of the passage. What is the photograph used as an example of? Explain your answer.

_____

_____

_____

_____

_____

14 Describe **two** changes that can be made when choosing food that would be good for the environment.

1: _____

_____

2: _____

_____

15. The author wrote the passage to encourage readers to make small changes that will reduce climate change. Do you think the author does a good job of convincing readers to change? If yes, explain what you think the author did well. If not, explain what you think the author could have done better.

Practice Set 9

Interview

Journey to the Deep Ocean

Instructions

This set has one passage for you to read. The passage is followed by questions.

Read each question carefully. For each multiple choice question, fill in the circle for the correct answer. For other types of questions, follow the instructions given. Some of the questions require a written answer. Write your answer on the lines provided.

Journey to the Deep Ocean
A Fictional Interview with James Cameron

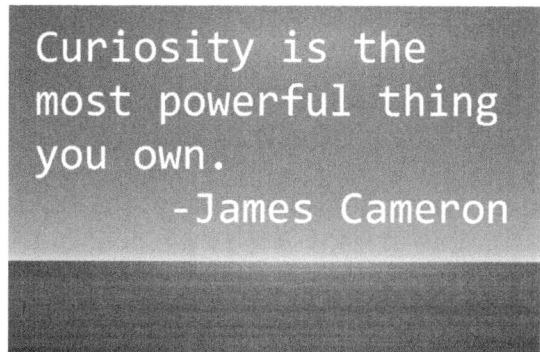

Background

James Cameron is a famous film director. He has made many well-known films. James is also an explorer and adventurer. In 2012, he traveled to the deepest part of the ocean in a special submarine. The deepest part of the ocean is known as the Mariana Trench. It is off the coast of Guam, in the western Pacific Ocean. To reach the bottom of the Mariana Trench, he would have to dive down around 36,000 feet. James wanted to explore and see what he could find down there. He also wanted to collect data for scientific analysis.

We interviewed James about that event. He gave us some personal insight into that most intriguing journey – the journey to the bottom of the ocean.

Interview

Interviewer: We would like to welcome film director, explorer, and adventurer, James Cameron, to the show. Welcome, James. It's a pleasure to have you with us today. How are you?

James: I'm great. Thank you for having me on the show. It's a pleasure to be here.

Interviewer: So, James. We're all very interested to hear about your journey to the deepest part of the ocean. Could you briefly tell us what motivated you to do something like that?

James: I have always dreamed of diving to the bottom of the ocean. Even as a little boy, I was curious about what lies down there. I realized, too, that we know more about the surface of Mars than the deepest part of the ocean. Being an explorer and scientist at heart, I thought, "Why is this so? Why not go down there and have a look and try to learn more about it? We may be able to discover some interesting things about our oceans."

Interviewer: I see. A mix of curiosity and searching for knowledge. So, you designed and built a special submarine to enable you to go down there. Tell us a little bit about that submarine.

James: The submarine was named the *Deepsea Challenger*. It was designed to be driven by one person only. It was also designed to handle the immense pressure at the bottom of the ocean. If it was not super strong, it would have caved in and I would have died instantly. The vessel was fitted with oxygen systems to keep me alive. It was also fitted with equipment to move it around and collect samples. We installed specially designed cameras to take video footage.

Interviewer: Are there any other challenges that the design team had to overcome?

James: There is no sunlight at the bottom of the ocean. So, we needed bright lights to be fitted to the inside and outside of the vessel.

Interviewer: Sounds awesome! A truly purpose-built vessel. So, give us a quick run-down of the journey. How long did it take? Were there any problems along the way?

James: To get to the bottom, it took about two and a half hours. Once there, I had planned to spend six hours collecting samples and taking video footage of the surroundings. Unfortunately, I ran into some trouble at the bottom, which forced me to come back to the surface earlier than planned.

Interviewer: Oh no! What happened down there?

James: Well, I'm talking to you now, so it wasn't life-threatening! There was a fluid leak. The fluid covered the pilot viewing window. That made it hard to see and drive the submarine. There were also some other faults that made it hard to collect samples. Given that it was hard to see and I could no longer collect samples, I thought it best to return to the surface.

Interviewer: So, you decided to come back up. How long did the return journey take?

James: The return journey took about 70 minutes. It was actually a lot faster than we all expected.

Interviewer: I'm guessing you were feeling a little disappointed that you had to return early.

James: Of course. But these things happen. The submarine was designed and built from scratch. There will always be something that fails on the day. We still managed to get some excellent footage and lots of samples. We'll just have to go down there again to collect more.

Interviewer: What happened when you returned to the surface?

James: When I reached the surface, a helicopter was sent to find me. Then a research ship came and pulled me out of the water. It was great to be back safe and well.

Interviewer: OK, so there is one question that I think all our viewers would love to ask you. Just what did you see down there? Many weird and wonderful creatures?

James: When I reached the bottom, I landed on a very flat, soft plain. I then began to drive the submarine around the area. The amazing thing is that I didn't see any fish or other creatures more than an inch long down there. I only saw small, shrimplike creatures. These are fairly common and I wasn't surprised to see them. I honestly thought I would see more life down there.

Interviewer: And finally, were you scared? You can be honest.

James: I guess at first, I was. When I was climbing into the submarine, I had butterflies in my stomach. However, I had faith in the quality of the vessel. I felt it had been designed and built well. Once I got into the pilot seat, I was confident that it would do the job. I also felt excited to be going to a place so inaccessible to most people.

Interviewer: Thank you for your comments. It has been exciting to talk with you about that most interesting trip. An amazing adventure and an outstanding achievement.

James: My pleasure. Again, thanks for having me.

© Angela George, Wikimedia Commons

James Cameron is known around the world as a film director. He wrote and directed famous films including *Terminator*, *Titanic*, and *Avatar*. He has won Golden Globe Awards, Academy Awards, and has a star on the Hollywood Walk of Fame. Many people do not realize that his achievements in exploration are just as impressive as his achievements in film.

Reading Skills Workbook, Focus on Nonfiction, Grade 5

1 Read this sentence from the passage.

> **He gave us some personal insight into that most intriguing journey – the journey to the bottom of the ocean.**

The word *intriguing* means that the journey was –

- Ⓐ very dangerous
- Ⓑ very interesting
- Ⓒ very serious
- Ⓓ very unusual

2 Complete the details below to list facts about the Mariana Trench.

Country located next to: _____

Ocean located in: _____

Distance to the bottom: _____

3 What is the first question about the journey the interviewer asks James?

- Ⓐ why he chose to do it
- Ⓑ what he discovered
- Ⓒ how it felt to get there
- Ⓓ how much it cost

4 In which sentence from paragraph 7 is the interviewer summarizing what James said?

Ⓐ   *I see.*

Ⓑ   *A mix of curiosity and searching for knowledge.*

Ⓒ   *So, you designed and built a submarine to enable you to go down there.*

Ⓓ   *Tell us a little bit about that submarine.*

5 Complete the table below by listing how the submarine solved each problem related to the deep ocean.

Problem	Solution
There is high pressure.	
There is no oxygen.	
There is no light.	

6 Select the **two** sentences that describe features of the *Deepsea Challenger* that would have allowed it to collect data and information to share with others.

☐   It was designed to be driven by one person only.

☐   It was also designed to handle the immense pressure at the bottom of the ocean.

☐   The vessel was fitted with oxygen systems to keep me alive.

☐   It was also fitted with equipment to move it around and collect samples.

☐   We installed specially designed cameras to take video footage.

☐   So, we needed bright lights to be fitted to the inside and outside of the vessel.

7 Read this statement from the passage.

> **Interviewer: Oh no! What happened down there?**

How would the interviewer most likely sound when making this statement?

- Ⓐ amused
- Ⓑ concerned
- Ⓒ puzzled
- Ⓓ relaxed

8 In which sentence from paragraph 18 does James describe a positive outcome of the journey?

- Ⓐ *The submarine was designed and built from scratch.*
- Ⓑ *There will always be something that fails on the day.*
- Ⓒ *We still managed to get some excellent footage and lots of samples.*
- Ⓓ *We'll just have to go down there again to collect more.*

9 Describe **two** reasons given in the first paragraph that tell why James wanted to reach the bottom of the Mariana Trench.

1: _____

_____

2: _____

_____

10 How does the quote at the beginning of the passage help explain James Cameron's interest in exploring the deep ocean? Explain your answer.

_____

_____

_____

_____

_____

11 Read this statement made by James.

> **I realized, too, that we know more about the surface of Mars than the deepest part of the ocean.**

How does James most likely feel about this fact? Use details from the passage to support your answer.

_____

_____

_____

_____

12. Why did James return to the surface earlier than he expected? Use **two** details from the passage in your answer.

13. James states that "when I was climbing into the submarine, I had butterflies in my stomach." What does this statement mean? Explain your answer.

14. Based on the information in the third last paragraph, list **two** reasons James felt safe in the *Deepsea Challenger* submarine.

   1: _____

   2: _____

15 The journey was a success, but it was also disappointing in some ways. Describe **two** ways the journey was disappointing. Use at least **three** details from the passage to support your answer.

Practice Set 10

History Article

The First Moon Landing

Instructions
This set has one passage for you to read. The passage is followed by questions. Read each question carefully. For each multiple choice question, fill in the circle for the correct answer. For other types of questions, follow the instructions given. Some of the questions require a written answer. Write your answer on the lines provided.

The First Moon Landing

Mankind first landed on the Moon on July 20, 1969. This was an important day in human history. Mankind had been into space before, but not to the Moon.

In 1961, John. F. Kennedy was the American President. He made a famous promise to get man to the Moon by the end of the 1960s. He made that promise in a famous speech to Congress in May, 1961. Part of that speech is quoted below.

"First, I believe that this nation should commit itself to achieving the goal, before this decade is out, of landing a man on the Moon and returning him safely to the Earth. No single space project in this period will be more impressive to mankind, or more important for the long-range exploration of space; and none will be so difficult or expensive to accomplish."

In his speech, Kennedy asked for the support of Congress and for the huge amount of money needed to achieve the goal. The years following that speech were spent trying to make it happen. He had promised that the goal would be achieved by the end of the decade. Suddenly, that day was fast approaching. Many doubted if they would succeed in time.

The successful mission was known as Apollo 11. Why Apollo 11? There were many Apollo missions before this attempt to reach the Moon. Each one tested part of what would be required for Apollo 11 to put a person on the Moon. For example, Apollo 4 was the first test flight of the Saturn V rocket that would launch the astronauts into space. Apollo 7 was the first manned mission, and Apollo 8 was the first to reach and orbit the Moon. Apollo 10 was a practice for the real Moon landing, except the astronauts traveled down near the Moon without actually trying to land. All these steps, and many more, were necessary for the Moon landing to be possible.

Finally, Apollo 11 would attempt to land a person on the Moon. On the Apollo 11 mission were astronauts Neil Armstrong, Buzz Aldrin, and Michael Collins. On the morning of July 16, 1969, these three men lifted off from the Kennedy Space Center. They left at 9:32 and just twelve minutes later were out of the Earth's atmosphere.

Three days later, on July 19, the crew were in the Moon's orbit. A day after that, Armstrong and Aldrin got into the lunar module named *Eagle* and prepared for descent. Collins remained in orbit in the control module named *Columbia*. Armstrong and Aldrin successfully landed *Eagle* on the Moon's surface at 3:17 p.m. on July 20.

Later that evening, Armstrong was ready to climb out of *Eagle* and walk on the Moon's surface. Around one billion people watched this event unfold on their television sets. Armstrong climbed down the ladder and placed his foot on the surface. At 9:56 p.m. on July 20, Armstrong became the first person to step on the surface of the Moon. He famously said, "That's one small step for a man, one giant leap for mankind."

Aldrin then joined Armstrong on the surface of the Moon. They spent two hours collecting samples. In those two hours, they also took photos. They put an American flag on the surface of the Moon. Armstrong and Aldrin then returned to *Eagle*. They blasted off, heading for the control module. Collins was thrilled to see them when they returned to *Columbia*.

The full crew then returned to Earth. They dropped into the Pacific Ocean near Hawaii on July 24, 1969. They had successfully landed on the Moon and returned safely. Over the next three and a half years, more astronauts would make this journey. Ten more would reach the Moon's surface. The first Moon landing was an outstanding achievement for scientists and engineers. It paved the way for future space exploration.

America had set an ambitious goal. It took dedication and a great deal of effort, resources, and money to achieve it. Neil Armstrong is remembered as the first person to step on the Moon, but he did not do it alone. It took thousands of people to make it happen. In the moment that Neil Armstrong stepped on the Moon, people from all around the world were amazed and inspired by what people could achieve.

Fun Fact

There is no atmosphere on the Moon, and so no wind. A flag placed on the Moon would not flutter in the breeze. Instead, it would flop down sadly next to the flagpole. This was not the sort of image NASA wanted to send all around the world!

The flag that Neil Armstrong placed on the Moon had wire in the top and bottom. This made it appear like it was flying proudly in the wind.

1   Read these sentences from the passage.

> **This was an important day in human history. Mankind had been into space before, but not to the Moon.**

How is the second sentence related to the claim in the first sentence?

- Ⓐ   It gives details to support the claim.
- Ⓑ   It restates the claim in a different way.
- Ⓒ   It tells who made the claim.
- Ⓓ   It gives an argument against the claim.

2   Read these sentences from the passage.

> **He had promised that the goal would be achieved by the end of the decade. Suddenly, that day was fast approaching. Many doubted if they would succeed in time.**

These sentences mainly create a sense of —

- Ⓐ   confidence
- Ⓑ   curiosity
- Ⓒ   excitement
- Ⓓ   worry

3   The passage describes how Armstrong "placed his foot on the surface." The word *placed* suggests that he put his foot down —

- Ⓐ   eagerly
- Ⓑ   gently
- Ⓒ   roughly
- Ⓓ   suddenly

4 Which sentence from paragraph 8 best shows how interested people were in the Moon landing?

Ⓐ   *Later that evening, Armstrong was ready to climb out of* Eagle *and walk on the Moon's surface.*

Ⓑ   *Around one billion people watched this event unfold on their television sets.*

Ⓒ   *Armstrong climbed down the ladder and placed his foot on the surface.*

Ⓓ   *He famously said, "That's one small step for a man, one giant leap for mankind."*

5 Read these sentences from the last paragraph.

> **Neil Armstrong is remembered as the first person to step on the Moon, but he did not do it alone. It took thousands of people to make it happen.**

These sentences have a message about –

Ⓐ   courage

Ⓑ   hope

Ⓒ   patience

Ⓓ   teamwork

6 Summarize the achievements of the three astronauts by selecting **all** the correct boxes.

	Neil Armstrong	**Buzz Aldrin**	**Michael Collins**
Was part of the Apollo 11 mission	☐	☐	☐
Stood on the surface of the Moon	☐	☐	☐
Became the first person to step onto the Moon	☐	☐	☐

7 Circle the **two** phrases from John F. Kennedy's speech that best show why he considered that putting a person on the Moon was a worthy goal.

> First, I believe that this nation should commit itself to achieving the goal, before this decade is out, of landing a man on the Moon and returning him safely to the Earth. No single space project in this period will be more impressive to mankind, or more important for the long-range exploration of space; and none will be so difficult or expensive to accomplish.

8 Paragraph 5 describes the missions that occurred before Apollo 11. What does this information show about the amount of preparation needed for Apollo 11? Use **two** details from the paragraph to support your answer.

_____

_____

_____

_____

9   The passage describes the two parts of the spacecraft, *Eagle* and *Columbia*. List what each part was and what its role was.

   Eagle: _____

   _____

   Columbia: _____

   _____

10   Complete the web below by listing **three** things that Armstrong did while on the Moon.

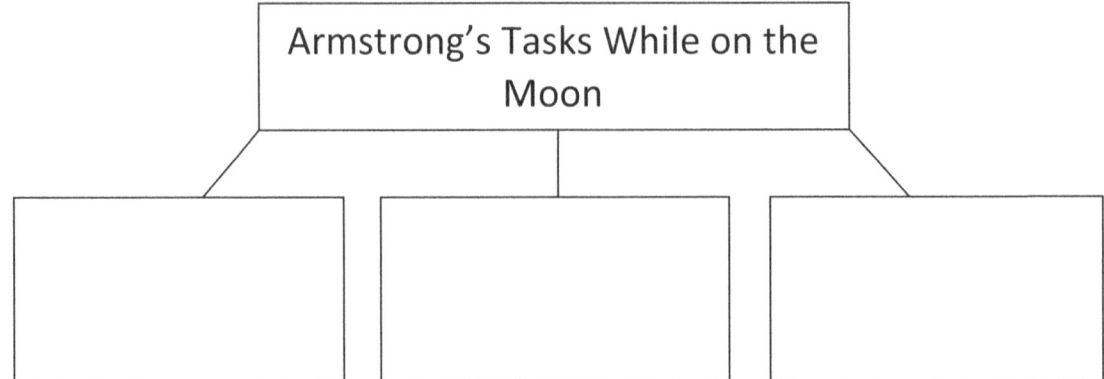

11   The passage states that Collins was thrilled to see Armstrong and Aldrin when they returned to *Columbia*. Why do you think Collins was thrilled? Explain your answer.

_____

_____

_____

_____

_____

12   Why was wire put in the flag placed on the Moon? Use **two** details from the passage to support your answer.

_____

_____

_____

_____

_____

13 Complete the missing entries on the timeline below by summarizing the event that took place at each time.

July 16, 9:32 a.m. *Apollo 11 launched*

July 19 _____

July 20, 3:17 p.m. _____

July 20, 9:56 p.m. _____

July 24 *Apollo 11 returned to Earth*

14 Describe **two** effects of the Moon landing described in the second last paragraph.

1. _____

_____

2. _____

_____

15. How does the author suggest that the first Moon landing is something that all Americans should be proud of? Use details from the passage to support your answer.

Practice Set 11

Flyers

Set of Three Flyers

Instructions

This set has several passages for you to read. Each passage is followed by questions.

Read each question carefully. For each multiple choice question, fill in the circle for the correct answer. For other types of questions, follow the instructions given. Some of the questions require a written answer. Write your answer on the lines provided.

Tennis Camp

Samuel is a talented tennis player and hopes to become a professional tennis player one day. In the summer, Samuel is attending the Tennis Summer Camp described in the flyer below.

1. According to the flyer, about how long does the tennis camp go for?

    Ⓐ 1 day

    Ⓑ 1 week

    Ⓒ 1 month

    Ⓓ 1 summer

2. At the end of the camp, who will players compete against in the William's Cup Tennis Contest?

    Ⓐ the coaches and trainers

    Ⓑ professional tennis players

    Ⓒ other players in the same age group

    Ⓓ other players of about the same ability

3. Which words from the section of the flyer titled "Skills Training" emphasize the effectiveness of the drills?

    Ⓐ "daily training drills"

    Ⓑ "forehand, backhand, and serving"

    Ⓒ "developed by professionals"

    Ⓓ "see fast improvements"

4   Which of the following is the main purpose of the tennis camp overall?

   Ⓐ   to make good tennis players even better

   Ⓑ   to introduce students to the sport of tennis

   Ⓒ   to inspire people to become professional tennis players

   Ⓓ   to show the importance of hard work and sacrifice

5   Describe **two** details from the passage that support your answer to Question 4.

   1: _____

   _____

   2: _____

   _____

6   The flyer states that students at the camp will "learn from the best." How does the author support this idea? Use **two** details from the flyer in your response.

   _____

   _____

   _____

   _____

Cameron's Photography Courses

Cameron has been a professional photographer for 15 years. He first started taking photographs as a kid, and it soon became a serious hobby. Finally, it became his full-time job. Cameron's work has been published all around the world and he has won many awards. He is especially famous for taking photographs of birds and other wildlife.

Recently, Cameron decided to start running his own youth training courses to share his passion and experience with others. His courses are held after school and are designed for students from 10 to 16. Cameron created the flyer below to promote his new business.

1 Which detail from the passage would be best to add to the flyer to give readers practical information on the courses?

- Ⓐ why Cameron started the courses
- Ⓑ when and where the courses are held
- Ⓒ what Cameron wants to teach students
- Ⓓ how long Cameron has been running the courses for

2 Read the following phrase from the flyer.

> **Ready. Set. Wow!**

Which statement describes the main purpose of the phrase?

- Ⓐ to explain the importance of preparation and planning
- Ⓑ to suggest that taking great photographs is easy
- Ⓒ to create a sense of excitement about what people might capture
- Ⓓ to show that the patience required will be worth it

3 Read this statement from the flyer.

> **A camera will put a world of possibilities at your fingertips.**

Explain what this statement means. In your answer, describe what Cameron is trying to get students excited about.

_____

_____

_____

_____

4   Describe **two** details from the passage that suggest that Cameron has the knowledge and experience to teach photography.

   1: _____

   _____

   2: _____

   _____

5   The passage describes Cameron as being famous for his photographs of birds and other wildlife. How does the illustration of the photographer in the flyer relate to this idea?

   _____

   _____

   _____

   _____

6   Does the style and art of the flyer make Cameron's classes seem serious or fun? Explain your answer.

   _____

   _____

   _____

   _____

   _____

   _____

The Circus is Coming to Town

Annabelle was excited to find this flyer in her local newspaper.

1. The flyer states that the circus includes a "Hercules Man." A "Hercules Man" is most likely someone who is –

   Ⓐ athletic

   Ⓑ daring

   Ⓒ mysterious

   Ⓓ strong

2. Which statement from the flyer directs people to take action? Select the **one** correct answer.

   ☐ Magical Mystery Show!

   ☐ Amazing Show

   ☐ 16th May, 19 pm

   ☐ Amazing Acrobats

   ☐ See It to Believe It

   ☐ Get Your Tickets Now

3. Which statement could be added to the end of the flyer to give readers a sense of urgency?

   Ⓐ Tickets Selling Fast and Will Sell Out!

   Ⓑ Discount Family Tickets Available

   Ⓒ Only $10 Per Adult and $5 Per Child

   Ⓓ Gold Passes Give You Backstage Access

4. The phrase "See It to Believe It" suggests that the circus will amaze people. Which act mentioned in the flyer do you think would be most amazing? Explain why you chose that act.

_____

_____

_____

_____

_____

5. Which detail in the flyer shows that the circus has been held many times before? Explain your answer.

_____

_____

_____

_____

6. How does the art in the flyer make the circus seem fun and exciting? Give **two** specific examples from the flyer.

1: _____

_____

2: _____

_____

Practice Set 12

Advertisements

Set of Three Advertisements

Instructions

This set has several passages for you to read. Each passage is followed by questions.

Read each question carefully. For each multiple choice question, fill in the circle for the correct answer. For other types of questions, follow the instructions given. Some of the questions require a written answer. Write your answer on the lines provided.

Farm Fresh Tomato Sauce

Zoe's family have been making tomato sauce and other similar products for generations. There current product range includes all of the following:

- spicy chili and tomato ketchup
- basil and herb pasta sauce
- roasted garlic pasta sauce
- herby pizza sauce
- tomato and capsicum dip
- sundried tomato dip

The picture below shows an advertisement that runs for their original and still their best-selling product.

1 Read this statement from the advertisement.

> **Ideal with all dishes.**

Which word means about the same as *ideal*?

- Ⓐ   clever
- Ⓑ   delicious
- Ⓒ   matched
- Ⓓ   perfect

2 The advertisement describes the product as a "premium tomato sauce." This means that the tomato sauce is –

- Ⓐ   better quality than others
- Ⓑ   cheaper than others
- Ⓒ   more popular than others
- Ⓓ   stronger than others

3 Describe **two** ways the art in the advertisement emphasizes that the product is made from real tomatoes.

1: _____

_____

2: _____

_____

4   The first paragraph and the advertisement both show that the product has a long history. Complete the table by listing the detail from the first paragraph and the advertisement that shows this.

Details Showing the Long History of the Product

Section	Detail
First paragraph	
Advertisement	

5   Contrast the product in the advertisement with the products listed in the passage. Describe **two** ways the product in the advertisement is different.

_____

_____

_____

_____

6   Do you think the art in the background of the advertisement helps sell the product? Explain why or why not.

_____

_____

_____

_____

Durian Food Products

It looks strange. It smells strange. It tastes strange. It even has a strange history. Durian is certainly an exotic fruit with a difference.

Durian often divides people. Some people find the odor sweet and delicious, while others find it overpowering and disgusting. It has even been described as smelling like stinky socks. In fact, the odor is so strong that durians are banned on Singapore subways. And once, an aircraft carrying a crate of durian was delayed from taking off when the passengers complained of the smell filling the cabin!

It's difficult to describe the taste. There is a sense of sweet caramel, but also hints of onion and garlic. Maybe you just have to taste it to understand it. Many people who taste it become obsessed with it. Fans of the fruit describe it as the greatest taste on earth.

Luckily, our products make trying durian easy. We have made this tricky fruit into a wide variety of products that make the most of the unique flavor. You won't be overwhelmed by our products. They are subtle, balanced, and ready for you to enjoy for breakfast, as snacks, or in baking.

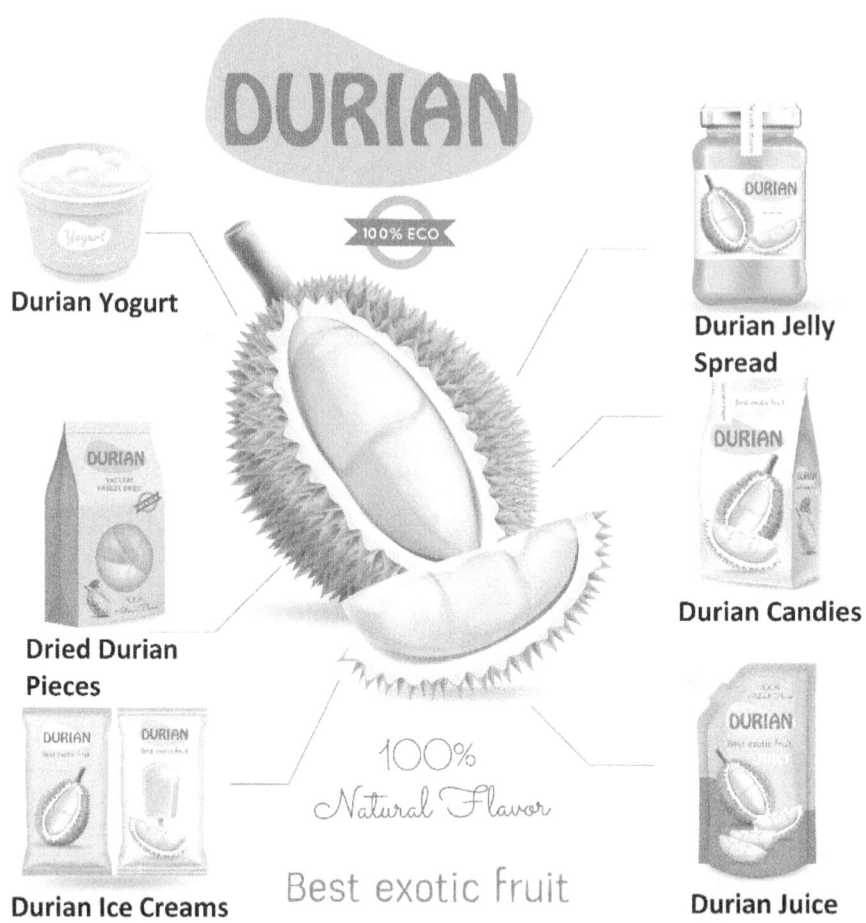

1. Which sentence about durian from the first paragraph is supported by the advertisement?

   Ⓐ   It looks strange.

   Ⓑ   It smells strange.

   Ⓒ   It tastes strange.

   Ⓓ   It even has a strange history.

2. Describe **two** examples the author gives in the passage to emphasize how strong the smell of durian is.

   1: _____

   _____

   2: _____

   _____

3. The passage states that there are durian products available "to enjoy for breakfast, as snacks, or in baking." Complete the web below by listing the **three** products that would be most suitable for breakfast.

```
                    Durian Breakfast Products
           ┌──────────────┬──────────────┬──────────────┐
           │              │              │              │
           └──────────────┴──────────────┴──────────────┘
```

4. How does the information in the advertisement support the idea that durian has been made into "a wide variety of products"? Explain your answer.

5. How do the products shown on the advertisement make it easier for people to try durian? Explain your answer.

6. Does the information in the passage make you curious about trying durian? Explain why or why not.

Summer Crush Smoothies

Pax's father sells fruit juices and smoothies at the local markets. Pax's father made this advertisement to promote his two new products that he is calling "Summer Crush."

1 The advertisement repeats the phrase "enjoy every sip" several times. This phrase mainly suggests enjoying the smoothies –

- Ⓐ slowly
- Ⓑ outdoors
- Ⓒ with friends
- Ⓓ for breakfast

2 What is the most likely reason the advertisement includes photographs of fruit?

- Ⓐ to suggest that people can design their own flavors
- Ⓑ to warn that each smoothie could contain seeds
- Ⓒ to show that each smoothie comes with a serving of fruit
- Ⓓ to emphasize that the smoothies are made with real fruit

3 The advertisement describes the smoothies as *seasonal* and *limited*. Explain what each word tells you about the smoothies.

seasonal: _____

_____

limited: _____

_____

4   Compare the two smoothies described in the advertisement. Describe **one** way they are similar and **one** way they are different.

    _____

    _____

    _____

    _____

    _____

5   Describe **two** ways the advertisement suggests that the smoothies would be a good choice on a hot summer day.

    1: _____

    _____

    2: _____

    _____

6   Do you think that "Summer Crush" is a good name for the products? Explain why you feel that way.

    _____

    _____

    _____

    _____

    _____

Practice Set 13

Science Article

Exploring the Deep

Instructions

This set has one passage for you to read. The passage is followed by questions.

Read each question carefully. For each multiple choice question, fill in the circle for the correct answer. For other types of questions, follow the instructions given. Some of the questions require a written answer. Write your answer on the lines provided.

Exploring the Deep

We have explored space. We have explored the jungles. We have explored the highest mountains. But there is still one place that we hardly know anything about: the deep ocean. Only a tiny part of the deep ocean has ever been explored. Explorers can only dive down a small way before the weight of the ocean becomes too great. Even with special diving gear there is so much pressure it is impossible for humans to get anywhere near the deep oceans. If you went down to the deepest point, it would feel like 50 jumbo jets were stacked up on top of you! So, because we just can't get down that far the deep ocean remained a mystery for thousands of years. I know what you're thinking. There must be some other way to explore the ocean, right? Explorers thought the same thing. And you're right. There is another way.

Scuba divers can use oxygen tanks to explore some parts of the ocean. But they cannot explore the deep ocean.

Meet D2. He makes it possible for people to explore the deep ocean. D2 is a robot. D2 might not be the kind of robot you are thinking of. D2 doesn't look like a person or walk around. Instead, D2 is a special type of vehicle that is a bit like a toy remote-control car. Like those toy cars, D2 can be controlled by someone far away. They call D2 a remotely operated vehicle, or an ROV. D2 also has cameras to film everything it sees. The person controlling D2 can explore what they want to and see everything that the camera sees on a screen. It is almost like they are there. Using D2, and other ROVs, explorers have been able to see deep down into the ocean. They have even seen into the deepest part, the Mariana Trench.

The Mariana Trench is located in the Pacific Ocean. It is found around 120 miles from the Mariana Islands. The Mariana Trench is deeper than any other part of the ocean. It drops down almost 7 miles. That's deeper than the Grand Canyon! The Mariana Trench is a huge area and is filled with mysterious creatures. You wouldn't believe some of the plants and animals that have been found down there. They really are quite strange! The strangest thing is that they can survive at such depths.

Plants and animals in the Mariana Trench have to survive under huge pressure from the water. They also have to survive without sunlight. The trench is completely dark. Scientists once believed that sunlight was needed to survive. They thought the cold, dark deep ocean would be as lifeless as the Moon. Surely nothing could survive under all of that pressure in the dark! But something did. Actually, explorers found lots of things living in the Mariana Trench. The water pressure and darkness seem to be no problem at all for these unusual deep ocean plants and animals.

One of the strangest creatures in the deep ocean are the incredible giant tube worms. These huge worms grow to over 8 feet long. They grow in groups. These groups of giant tube worms are quite a unique sight. And how they survive is just as unique. They have no sunlight to get energy from, so the tube worms survive using bacteria. Amazingly, the bacteria live inside the tube worm and make food for it. That's quite yucky to think about! So the bacteria are giving the tube worms food. But where, you might ask, do the bacteria get their own food from? Well, the bacteria feed off chemicals in the water. The tube worms live next to hot vents where there are lots of chemicals. These hot vents look like chimneys in the ocean floor. Imagine a chimney with hot black smoke pouring out. That's what the vents look like. The materials flowing out are not smoke, but are a mix of chemicals. The bacteria use these chemicals to make food, and the tube worms survive on this food. Now that's strange!

Another strange creature is the Dumbo octopus. Perhaps you're wondering what's so weird about an octopus. I bet you've seen or heard of lots of those. Well, the weird thing about this octopus is that it has big ears. Have you heard of Dumbo the Elephant? He had big floppy ears too. The Dumbo octopus's ears, flapping around in the water, make it one of the cutest strange creatures. Its body is a tiny 12 inches long. It has big eyes and floats around with its tentacles spread out like an umbrella. The Dumbo octopus is not just cute. It is strong too. It can survive thousands of feet below sea level. No other octopus species that we know about can live that deep.

Perhaps the most alien-like animals that live in the deep ocean are the ones that light up. On land it is pretty strange to glow. If you started glowing, people might get a fright! But there are many glowing creatures in the deep sea. In fact, one scientist says that almost all of the creatures living in the deep sea can make light. You might find glowing jellyfish, shrimps, squid, or a scary-looking dragonfish. Some of them light up and some shoot light out into the water like fireworks.

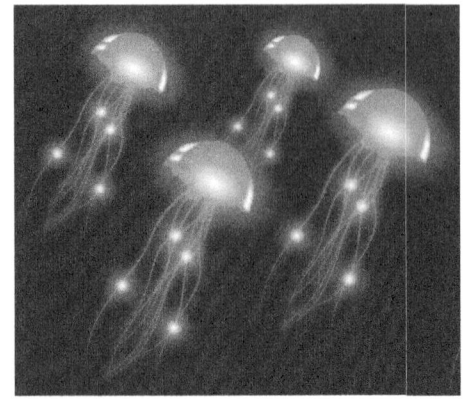

The deep sea is an untouched world. The more we explore it the more we see what an incredible place it is. It's incredible to imagine what we might discover next!

1 What is the main reason it is difficult to explore the deep ocean?

   Ⓐ   It is too dark.

   Ⓑ   The pressure is too great.

   Ⓒ   There are too many strange creatures.

   Ⓓ   It takes too long to reach the bottom.

2 Which sentence from the passage best supports your answer to Question 1?

   Ⓐ   *Only a tiny part of the deep ocean has ever been explored.*

   Ⓑ   *Explorers can only dive down a small way before the weight of the ocean becomes too great.*

   Ⓒ   *You wouldn't believe some of the plants and animals that have been found down there.*

   Ⓓ   *They thought the cold, dark deep ocean would be as lifeless as the Moon.*

3 Select **all** the sentences below that make a comparison.

   ☐   The Mariana Trench is located in the Pacific Ocean.

   ☐   It is found around 120 miles from the Mariana Islands.

   ☐   The Mariana Trench is deeper than any other part of the ocean.

   ☐   It drops down almost 7 miles.

   ☐   That's deeper than the Grand Canyon!

   ☐   The Mariana Trench is a huge area and is filled with mysterious creatures.

4 According to the passage, why do giant tube worms need bacteria?

- Ⓐ to give them food
- Ⓑ to provide light
- Ⓒ to keep them warm
- Ⓓ to use as shelter

5 Why are the hot vents in the ocean floor important for the survival of the giant tube worms?

- Ⓐ They heat the cold ocean water to a higher temperature.
- Ⓑ They help the giant tube worms hide from predators.
- Ⓒ They provide the chemicals that the bacteria need to make food.
- Ⓓ They allow the giant tube worms to remain together in groups.

6 The author describes the deep ocean plants and animals as being unusual. List **four** words the author uses when describing the creatures that mean about the same as *unusual*. Write the words on the lines.

1. _____

2. _____

3. _____

4. _____

7 Which statement below best describes the main idea of the passage?

   Ⓐ   The deep ocean is so deep that there is no light.

   Ⓑ   The deep ocean can be observed using robots.

   Ⓒ   The deep ocean is full of fascinating creatures.

   Ⓓ   The deep ocean has sea creatures that glow.

8 Based on your answer to Question 7, describe how the author uses examples to support the main idea.

_____

_____

_____

_____

9 How does the robot D2 allow explorers to study the deep ocean? Use **two** details from the passage to support your response.

_____

_____

_____

_____

10   Describe **two** reasons scientists first thought that no animals would be able to survive in the deep ocean.

   1: _____
   _____

   2: _____
   _____

11   Complete the web below by listing **three** details about the Dumbo octopus's appearance.

```
                    ┌─────────────────────────┐
                    │    The Dumbo Octopus    │
                    └─────────────────────────┘
                   /            │            \
        ┌──────────┐    ┌──────────┐    ┌──────────┐
        │          │    │          │    │          │
        │          │    │          │    │          │
        └──────────┘    └──────────┘    └──────────┘
```

12   List **two** things that make the Dumbo octopus different from other octopi.

   1: _____
   _____

   2: _____
   _____

13	Underline or highlight the simile in the paragraph below.

> **Perhaps the most alien-like animals that live in the deep ocean are the ones that light up. On land it is pretty strange to glow. If you started glowing, people might get a fright! But there are many glowing creatures in the deep sea. In fact, one scientist says that almost all of the creatures living in the deep sea can make light. You might find glowing jellyfish, shrimps, squid, or a scary-looking dragonfish. Some of them light up and some shoot light out into the water like fireworks.**

Describe what the simile you identified helps readers imagine.

_____

_____

14	The photograph at the start of the passage shows a scuba diver exploring the ocean. Why wouldn't a scuba diver be able to explore the deep ocean? Use **two** details from the passage to support your answer.

_____

_____

_____

_____

_____

15. How do you think scientists would have felt about what the learned when they first started exploring the deep ocean? Use **three** details from the passage to support your response.

Practice Set 14

Biography

Babe Ruth

Instructions

This set has one passage for you to read. The passage is followed by questions.

Read each question carefully. For each multiple choice question, fill in the circle for the correct answer. For other types of questions, follow the instructions given. Some of the questions require a written answer. Write your answer on the lines provided.

Babe Ruth

Babe Ruth was born on February 6, 1895, in Baltimore, Maryland. His birth name was George Herman Ruth Jr. However, he later came to be known as "Babe" Ruth. Babe's parents were George Herman Ruth Sr. and Kate Schamberger-Ruth. Babe was one of eight children.

Babe's family lived in a poor neighborhood. His parents owned a tavern and the family lived in rooms above it. His parents worked a lot. This meant they had little time to watch over their children. Babe would often skip school, steal things, and cause trouble.

His parents later decided that it would be best to send him to a boarding school. The St. Mary's Industrial School for Boys became Babe's home for 12 years. It was a place for children who had problems at home. The school was very strict.

Babe Ruth pitching for the Boston Red Sox, 1914.

The school's environment was exactly what Babe needed. One of the monks at the school, known as Brother Matthias, became a positive role model for Babe. Babe looked up to him like he would a father. Brother Matthias also taught Babe a lot about baseball. He helped him develop his skills and a love for the game.

By the age of 15, Babe was an exceptional baseball player. He was quite tall and very strong, making him a skillful and powerful player. One day, Jack Dunn, owner of the Baltimore Orioles, came to watch Babe play. After watching him play, Jack offered Babe a contract to come and play for his minor league team. This happened in February, 1914. Babe was only 19 years of age at the time. Babe was paid $600 for a 6-month contract. His teammates knew him as "Jack's newest babe." That's how George Herman Ruth Jr. came to be known as "Babe" Ruth.

Babe played well for the Orioles. He played so well that he was called up to the Boston Red Sox. He made his Major League debut on July 11, 1914. Over the next five years at the Boston Red Sox, Babe led the team to three championship victories. In the 1916 championship game, he pitched 13 scoreless innings in one game.

A statue honoring Babe Ruth stands outside the home of the Baltimore Orioles.

Aside from his pitching talent, he also demonstrated his skills with the bat. In the 1918 season, he hit 11 home runs. In the following year, 1919, he hit an amazing 29 home runs. Babe was developing into a true all-rounder.

Towards the end of 1919, the Boston Red Sox had some serious financial troubles. To raise much needed funds, Babe was sold to another team. On December 26, 1919, Babe left the Boston Red Sox and joined the New York Yankees. The Yankees paid $100,000 for Babe. At that time, that was a lot of money.

While playing for the Yankees, he continued to improve his game and break records. In the 1920 season, he hit 54 home runs. He beat his own record in the 1921 season, hitting a staggering 59 home runs.

Babe was a superstar of the game. At that time, the New York Yankees were a very dominant team. Many people came to watch Babe and the Yankees play. They wanted to see his talent for themselves.

In 1927, Babe hit a total 60 home runs in a season. That record stood for 34 years. Babe lifted his team to new heights. In fact, the 1927 New York Yankees team is still considered one of the best teams in history.

Babe retired from baseball in 1935. At that time, he was playing for the Boston Braves. He had a career home run total of 714. He is third on the 'most home runs in a season' list. In 1936, the Baseball Hall of Fame was created. Babe was one of the first five players to be added to the hall of fame.

Babe was known as a generous man. During his last years, he spent his time, resources, and energy helping charities. When he died, much of his money went to the Babe Ruth Foundation. This foundation was a charity set up to help underprivileged children. This money was very much appreciated.

Babe Ruth is still known as one of the greatest baseball players of all time. He set many records. Many people loved to watch him play. He provided hope to many who were going through difficult times during the Great Depression. He was a generous man who helped other people.

Even today, young baseball players look up to and admire Babe Ruth.

1   Read this sentence from the passage.

    Babe would often skip school, steal things, and cause trouble.

    What does the word *skip* mean in the sentence?
    - Ⓐ   Babe enjoyed school.
    - Ⓑ   Babe played sport in school.
    - Ⓒ   Babe did not attend school.
    - Ⓓ   Babe did poorly at school.

2   What is the most likely reason Babe's parents sent him to a boarding school?
    - Ⓐ   They wanted to improve his behavior.
    - Ⓑ   They needed more room at home.
    - Ⓒ   They hoped he would develop his baseball skills.
    - Ⓓ   They could not afford to care for him.

3   The passage describes how Babe "looked up to" Brother Matthias. This means that Babe –
    - Ⓐ   argued with him
    - Ⓑ   was afraid of him
    - Ⓒ   rebelled against him
    - Ⓓ   respected him

4   According to the passage, who gave Babe his famous nickname?

   Ⓐ   his parents

   Ⓑ   the media

   Ⓒ   Brother Matthias

   Ⓓ   his Baltimore Orioles' teammates

5   Which sentence from paragraph 5 represents the start of Babe's professional career?

   Ⓐ   *By the age of 15, Babe was an exceptional baseball player.*

   Ⓑ   *He was quite tall and very strong, making him a skillful and powerful player.*

   Ⓒ   *After watching him play, Jack offered Babe a contract to come and play for his team.*

   Ⓓ   *His teammates knew him as "Jack's newest babe."*

6   What does the statue of Babe Ruth suggest about how the Baltimore Orioles feel about him?

   Ⓐ   They are embarrassed they did not pay him enough.

   Ⓑ   They are annoyed they let him go to another team.

   Ⓒ   They are proud to have had him on their team.

   Ⓓ   They are impressed by his skills and his good character.

7 Read these sentences from the passage.

> **In 1927, Babe hit a total 60 homeruns in a season. That record stood for 34 years.**

How does the second sentence relate to the first?

- Ⓐ It suggests that it was a lucky season.
- Ⓑ It highlights how great the achievement was.
- Ⓒ It explains why Babe was so talented.
- Ⓓ It tells how Babe inspired others.

8 How did Brother Matthias affect Babe? Describe **two** ways he influenced Babe.

1: _____

_____

2: _____

_____

9 Complete the web below by listing **two** more of Babe's achievements while playing for the Boston Red Sox.

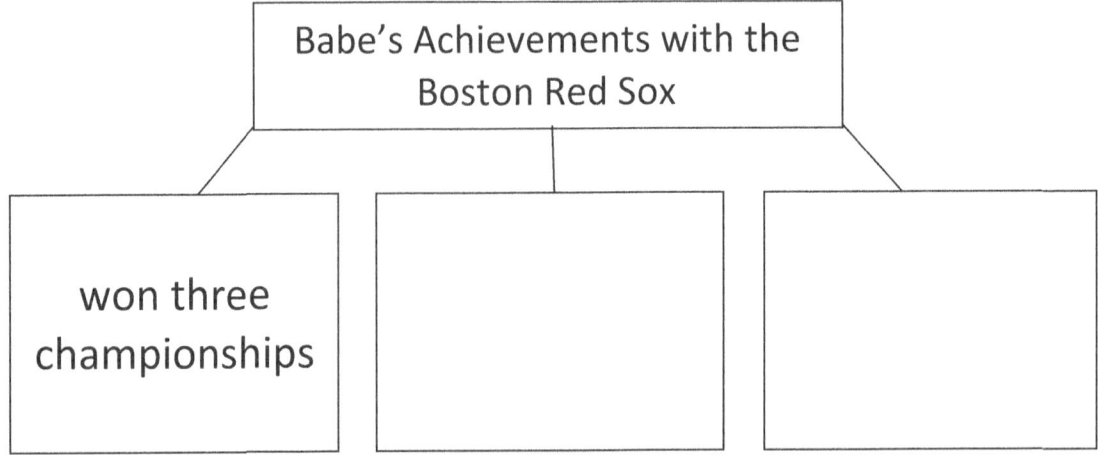

10   Explain why the Boston Red Sox let Babe Ruth go. Use **two** details from the passage to support your answer.

_____

_____

_____

_____

_____

_____

11   How does the author show that Babe made the Yankees more popular? Use **two** details from the passage to support your answer.

_____

_____

_____

_____

_____

_____

12 Complete the table below by listing the number of home runs Babe hit in each season.

Babe Ruth's Home Runs

Year	Number of Home Runs
1918	
1919	
1920	
1921	
1927	

13 What does the table completed in question 12 show about Babe Ruth? Explain your answer.

_____

_____

_____

_____

_____

14 Describe **two** details the author gives to support the idea that Babe was generous.

1: _____

_____

2: _____

_____

15 Write a short essay that supports the statement below.

> **Babe Ruth's achievements have not been forgotten.**

Use details from the passage in your response.

Practice Set 15

How-To Article

How to Write a Short Story

> **Instructions**
>
> This set has one passage for you to read. The passage is followed by questions.
>
> Read each question carefully. For each multiple choice question, fill in the circle for the correct answer. For other types of questions, follow the instructions given. Some of the questions require a written answer. Write your answer on the lines provided.

How to Write a Short Story

The Writing Process

Writing is something that people of all ages can enjoy. You don't need expensive tools or special equipment – just a pad and paper will do. Writing is great for expressing yourself, getting creative, and becoming your own inventor. When we write, we create our own whole new world just through pen and paper. You can create anything you can imagine – fascinating people, strange events, and even entire new planets! If you want to write a short story, whether for fun or for school, there are several steps that are helpful to know! Before you can start to write, you will need to brainstorm (think of ideas) and make an outline (a guide to what your story will be about). Then you can begin writing! After writing, you will need to reread your writing, edit it, and perfect it.

Brainstorming

If you want to write a short story for school or for fun, first you need ideas! You can get ideas for writing almost anywhere! Take a walk in the park, the closest city, or stroll around a shopping mall or a local museum.

You also don't have to leave your home to get ideas either. You can get ideas from things or activities you have done, your hobbies, or from magazines, newspapers, and the Internet. Inspiration is all around, so just look and see for yourself where you can find inspiration!

Making an Outline

Once you have some ideas you will need to make an outline. An outline is a guide that will help you write. You can create different topics and under each topic, you can put your ideas. Outlines can be very simple or very thorough. Outlines can include character descriptions, information about the setting, and even information about each chapter or section that you will write. It's your decision how long or short you want your outline to be.

Sometimes writers do not use an outline and just begin writing. This is called freewriting. Freewriting helps writers to start thinking and get more ideas. Even when you think you have nothing to write about, when you start freewriting, you will have more ideas. Many people, however, like to use outlines because they are very helpful. Outlines help writers collect their thoughts and get started.

Starting to Write

Once you have your outline, you can begin writing. If you are using an outline, you will already know what you want to write about! Outlines make it easy for new writers to know where to start. Under each topic or headline, you can fill in your thoughts. All you need are words and a place to write! You can write in a notebook, on your computer, on even on your iPad or other device. Keep referring back to your outline to keep your writing focused and on track.

After you start writing, make sure that your ideas follow a pattern. For example, you cannot write about a character without introducing the character to your story. Read the following sentences:

On the mountain, Jason saw a young girl with long beautiful brown hair walking towards him, wearing a jean skirt. When the girl met him on the path, he asked her for her name. She told him her name was Jenny Jean.

The sentences above introduce the girl, Jenny Jean, to the story. Now the readers know the character's name, what she is wearing, and what she looks like.

Without an outline, the writing process can be confusing and frustrating.

Revising and Editing Process

Don't forget to reread what you wrote! The first time we write something, we just put our ideas on paper. When we read what we wrote we will find some things that don't make sense. The process of rereading and fixing our mistakes is called revising and editing. Every great writer or author rereads their own work and makes changes. This process helps the writer to find errors. Sometimes we find that we forgot to write something important. Sometimes when we write, we repeat ourselves. We can improve or make our story better by rereading, editing, and looking for problems with grammar and sentence structure.

Also, if you want to learn to write short stories well, consider writing with other people, or having someone else read your story. Other people can help us learn from our mistakes, and can help us understand what was good and what we need to fix! It can be hard to hear this honest feedback, but listening to it is how you can make your work better. Other people might even have new ideas or ways of looking at things that you had not thought of.

Keep Writing

To become a great writer, you have to keep writing! Write, write, and write some more! As you write, you will get better and better. You will also have more ideas and make fewer mistakes. Many great writers write every day for at least 30 minutes! Famous writers become famous because they have practiced! You can also consider keeping a daily journal. A journal can help you keep track of your ideas, thoughts, and personal experiences. In the end, if you enjoy writing, you only need an idea and a pen and paper! Grab your pen and get started writing!

1. Read this sentence from the passage.

   Outlines can be very simple or very thorough.

   Which word means about the same as *thorough*?
   - Ⓐ basic
   - Ⓑ detailed
   - Ⓒ smooth
   - Ⓓ useful

2. The photograph in the section "Brainstorming" probably refers to getting ideas from –
   - Ⓐ a park
   - Ⓑ a city
   - Ⓒ a mall
   - Ⓓ a museum

3. Which sentence from "Starting to Write" describes a main benefit of having an outline?
   - Ⓐ *Once you have your outline, you can begin writing.*
   - Ⓑ *Outlines make it easy for new writers to know where to start.*
   - Ⓒ *Under each topic or headline, you can fill in your thoughts.*
   - Ⓓ *All you need are words and a place to write!*

4 Which term best describes the paragraph in italics in the section "Starting to Write"?

   Ⓐ a definition
   Ⓑ a summary
   Ⓒ an example
   Ⓓ an instruction

5 As it is used in the passage, what does the word *reread* refer to?

   Ⓐ reading aloud
   Ⓑ reading something again
   Ⓒ reading someone else's work
   Ⓓ reading in a different way

6 Use lines to match each section of the passage with what it mainly describes.

Section	What it Mainly Describes
Brainstorming	creating writing
Making an Outline	generating ideas
Starting to Write	improving writing
Revising and Editing Process	planning writing

7 Read these sentences from the passage.

> **In the end, if you enjoy writing, you only need an idea and a pen and paper! Grab your pen and get started writing!**

These sentences are probably meant to make the reader feel –

Ⓐ curious

Ⓑ enthusiastic

Ⓒ patient

Ⓓ thoughtful

8 The author describes writers as becoming their own inventors. Describe how a writer is like an inventor. Use **two** details from the passage to support your response.

_____

_____

_____

_____

9 Describe **two** benefits of writing the author gives in the first paragraph.

1: _____

_____

2: _____

_____

10 How could freewriting also help with brainstorming? Use **two** details from the passage to support your response.

_____

_____

_____

_____

_____

11 Look at the photograph on the second page of the passage. How does the photograph show the importance of having an outline? Explain your answer.

_____

_____

_____

_____

_____

12 Based on the details in the passage, list **three** mistakes a writer might fix when revising and editing.

1: _____

2: _____

3: _____

13 Explain why letting other people help you is important during the revising and editing process. Use **two** details from the passage to support your response.

_____

_____

_____

_____

_____

_____

14 How does the author emphasize the importance of practice in the section "Keep Writing"? Describe **two** specific ways the author emphasizes the importance of practice.

1. _____

_____

_____

2. _____

_____

_____

15. Why is writing an outline an important step in the writing process? Explain how it would help writers create a good short story. Use at least **three** details from the passage to support your response.

Practice Set 16

Opinion Piece

Children and Cell Phones

Instructions

This set has one passage for you to read. The passage is followed by questions.

Read each question carefully. For each multiple choice question, fill in the circle for the correct answer. For other types of questions, follow the instructions given. Some of the questions require a written answer. Write your answer on the lines provided.

Children and Cell Phones

Margaret Peterson, a worried mother, wrote this letter to the editor about the issue of young children having cell phones.

Dear Editor,

Last Sunday I read your article about how parents are giving their children cell phones at a young age. In your article, you said that parents need to think about the consequences of giving our children phones. You wrote about how many kids have smartphones in their hands instead of a soccer ball or a basketball. You also wrote that parents need to take responsibility for this issue.

I could not agree more, but I also believe that all adults need to help solve this problem. Parents, community leaders, teachers, and other people in authority need to work together to fix this problem. First, I think it is important to decide what age is appropriate to give our children phones. I think there should also be guidelines about the use of phones. Perhaps schools should not allow cell phones in class or on the school grounds at all.

Kids today seem to feel like they could not survive without a phone. They fear they are missing out. Sadly, what they are really missing out on is a childhood. When we were children, we did not have cell phones. This was never a problem. Now our children are growing up attached to their phones. They stare into them instead of enjoying the real world around them!

My daughter is only 4 years old. She knows how to talk into my cell phone, but she doesn't know how to play hopscotch. Today, children don't play outside like they used to. There are some kids in our neighborhood that don't even know what hide-and-go-seek is. Hide-and-go-seek is one of the oldest and most classic outdoor games, but our kids don't know these games. Kids need to run outside and have fun. At the end of the day, they go to sleep happy and exhausted. When our children spend the entire day on their phones, they cannot sleep at night. Then at night, they want to stay up and play on their phones even more!

This is not just a problem. It is a crisis. Parents need to be more responsible for the amount of time children are playing on their phones. We need to limit the amount of time they are allowed to spend on their phones. I understand that our younger children are watching their older brothers and sisters play games on their phones, and then they want to play too. This is a problem because our young children are learning from their siblings.

The use of cell phones is also harming children's social skills. We are risking that our children will not know how to make friends. This is a skill that often develops as children play together. Sadly, playing on a phone is not the same. Children may also have more difficulty talking to other people their age. When children spend the whole day on their phones, they are not talking to each other. It is sad that these important skills may be overlooked.

Not only do children not know how to be kids, there are many dangers in allowing young children to have phones. Although parents can have control over the use of their child or children's phones, children can delete messages, phone calls, and entire phone apps. Letting young children have smartphones is too risky. Today, children open their own Facebook account at far too young an age. This is something we cannot allow. Smartphones allow children to keep secrets from their parents and their families. The fact is that there are too many things on the Internet that we cannot control! Young people need to be protected!

I think that we are in a dangerous time when technology is taking control of our families. Giving phones to our young children is also taking away the attention of our children. Families are spending less time together! That is certainly wrong. We need to spend time with each other and take care of each other. Smartphones are even causing parents to pay less attention to their children. Parents also need to remember to put their phones out of sight too!

Thank you for reading my letter. I hope you will share my letter of concern in the newspaper this week. I think you will agree that I have a reason to be worried! I hope that every parent, teacher, coach, or any other role model will think about this issue and what actions can be taken to make things better.

Sincerely,

Margaret Peterson

Children should be spending more time enjoying themselves outdoors.

1   What extra opinion does the author have in addition to the opinion of the Sunday article she refers to?

     Ⓐ   Children should not be given cell phones.

     Ⓑ   Parents need to be responsible for their children's use of cell phones.

     Ⓒ   There are consequences to giving a young child a cell phone.

     Ⓓ   All adults need to help solve the problems of children and cell phone use.

2   Look at the photograph next to the first paragraph. What does the photograph suggest people are doing when using phones and computers?

     Ⓐ   ignoring each other

     Ⓑ   competing with each other

     Ⓒ   arguing with each other

     Ⓓ   playing together

3   Based on your answer to Question 2, what does the art suggest?

     Ⓐ   Technology has many positive uses.

     Ⓑ   Kids today use technology to communicate.

     Ⓒ   Young people focus too much on technology.

     Ⓓ   Playing games using technology has replaced playing outdoors.

4 Read these sentences from the passage.

> **When we were children, we did not have cell phones. This was never a problem. Now our children are growing up attached to their phones. They stare into them instead of enjoying the real world around them!**

Which term best describes how the sentences are organized?

- Ⓐ chronological order
- Ⓑ cause and effect
- Ⓒ problem and solution
- Ⓓ compare and contrast

5 Which phrase from paragraph 3 best summarizes the author's main point in the paragraph?

- Ⓐ *could not survive without a phone*
- Ⓑ *really missing out on is a childhood*
- Ⓒ *we did not have cell phones*
- Ⓓ *our children are growing up*

6 Read these sentences from the passage.

> **This is not just a problem. It is a crisis.**

What is the main purpose of these sentences?

- Ⓐ to suggest that the problem can easily be solved
- Ⓑ to show that the issue is not serious
- Ⓒ to highlight that things will continue to change
- Ⓓ to emphasize how great the problem is

7 Read this sentence form the passage.

Letting young children have smartphones is too risky.

What does the word *risky* mean?

- Ⓐ dangerous
- Ⓑ exciting
- Ⓒ fun
- Ⓓ serious

8 In the first paragraph, the author describes how the article wrote about how kids "have smartphones in their hands instead of a soccer ball or a basketball." What main problem does this statement describe? Explain your answer.

_____

_____

_____

_____

9 List **two** children's games the author mentions and the point she makes about each game.

1: _____

_____

2: _____

_____

10   Based on the passage, how is sleep different for people using phones all day than for people playing outside all day? Use **two** details from the passage in your answer.

_____
_____
_____
_____
_____

11   What example does the author give to show that siblings can be bad role models for their younger brothers or sisters? Use **two** details from the passage in your answer.

_____
_____
_____
_____
_____

12   According to the author, in what **two** ways do the use of cell phones harm young people's social skills?

1: _____

_____

2: _____

_____

13. What does the last paragraph of the passage show about who the author wants to influence with the letter? What does the author want these readers to do? Explain your answer.

14. Look at the photograph at the end of the passage. What does the photograph suggest about how kids feel when playing outdoors instead of playing on their phones? Explain your answer.

15 Do you agree with the author that children having cell phones is a serious problem? Explain why or why not. You can use details from the passage or your own ideas to support your answer.

Practice Set 17

History Article

The Hanging Gardens of Babylon

Instructions
This set has one passage for you to read. The passage is followed by questions. Read each question carefully. For each multiple choice question, fill in the circle for the correct answer. For other types of questions, follow the instructions given. Some of the questions require a written answer. Write your answer on the lines provided.

The Hanging Gardens of Babylon

The Hanging Gardens of Babylon is one of the Seven Wonders of the Ancient World. The Seven Wonders are ancient structures that are considered to be remarkable. They were remarkable for the time they were built, and many would still be marveled over if they were built today. These structures are all over 2,000 years old, and one is over 4,000 years old. Amazingly, the oldest of the Ancient Wonders is the only one that still exists today. It is the Great Pyramid of Giza and it still stands in Egypt. The Hanging Gardens of Babylon are interesting for a very different reason – they may not have existed at all!

There is no debating that the Great Pyramid of Giza is real. You can still visit it today! Proving that a garden existed over 2,000 years ago is a little trickier.

The Hanging Gardens of Babylon is the only one of the Seven Wonders of the World that may not have actually existed. Historians and other researchers are still debating whether the gardens were real. They have been described in ancient texts, but no solid evidence has ever been found to prove that they were real. It is possible that they were an idea of a stunning and impressive garden and more of a legend than anything that was ever actually built. It is still part of the Seven Wonders because it is currently accepted that the gardens were real, but were destroyed. However, this conclusion is not supported by all experts.

It is known as the Hanging Gardens because the gardens were built high on different levels of stone terraces. It was described as the most beautiful man-made gardens. The gardens also had flowers, fruits, waterfalls, and exotic creatures. It is also said that there were massive vaults and arches inside it.

Roman and Greek writers have written about the gardens in many classic works. Not all the writers agreed on why they were built or who built them. A popular idea is that the gardens were made by King Nebuchadnezzar II. He made the Hanging Gardens to make his wife happier. It is said that she missed the greenery and the rolling hills of her homeland. He made the greenery come to her by creating the gardens for her to admire. This idea is suggested because the gardens are thought to have been near the king and his wife's royal palace.

Another idea was that Queen Semiramis built the gardens. Queen Semiramis married an Assyrian king, and then took over leadership when he died a few years later. Greek texts tell of how one of her focuses was on completing new building projects. This included building the city of Babylon. The Greek texts describe how she built the city walls, temples, and the royal palace. Not everyone believes that this really happened, especially because Babylon is thought to have been founded before her time. However, if it did, it is possible that she also built the Hanging Gardens of Babylon.

Historians cannot even agree on the location of the gardens. There is another theory that the gardens may actually have been in Iraq. Nineveh is an ancient city located in modern-day Iraq. It is known that King Sennacherib had amazing gardens surrounding his palace in Nineveh. It is thought that over the years, the location may have become confused. Travelers may have reported the gardens as being in Babylon and could have exaggerated their features. A real garden that was quite impressive could have become a story about a wondrous structure.

> **Where's the Evidence?**
>
> If the gardens were real, why is there no evidence? Why have archaeologists never found any stones, arches, or aqueducts? One answer is that they may be buried under where the Euphrates River now flows. The ground under the river has not yet been able to be explored. The remains of the gardens could be there just waiting to be discovered.

The gardens were said to be 400 feet by 400 feet long. That is just over the size of three complete football fields. Watering such a huge area of plants would take over 8,000 gallons of water every single day! They were raised 75 feet high. Because the gardens were so high, the water would need to be carried up before you can water them. There would have had to be a complex irrigation system of canals, channels, pipes, and aqueducts.

The Hanging Gardens of Babylon are still being debated. There is not enough proof that they really existed. They may have been real, or they could also be a myth. It may never be known whether it was ever real, or is purely a wonderful work of fiction.

This picture shows what the Hanging Gardens of Babylon are thought to have looked like. As you can see, the plants did not really hang. Instead, they were built on different levels.

1 Read this sentence from the passage.

> **They were remarkable for the time they were built, and many would still be marveled over if they were built today.**

The phrase "marveled over" mainly suggests that people would –

- Ⓐ be amazed by the gardens
- Ⓑ feel curious about the gardens
- Ⓒ want to visit the gardens
- Ⓓ study the gardens closely

2 Which sentence from the first paragraph gives the main idea of the passage?

- Ⓐ *The Seven Wonders are ancient structures that are considered to be remarkable.*
- Ⓑ *They were remarkable for the time they were built, and many would still be marveled over if they were built today.*
- Ⓒ *These structures are all over 2,000 years old, and one is over 4,000 years old.*
- Ⓓ *The Hanging Gardens of Babylon are interesting for a very different reason – they may not have existed at all!*

3 Which word best describes the tone of the photograph's caption on the first page?

- Ⓐ admiring
- Ⓑ irritated
- Ⓒ light-hearted
- Ⓓ uncertain

4   Select the **two** sentences from paragraph 2 that best show that there are disagreements among researchers about the Hanging Gardens of Babylon.

☐   The Hanging Gardens of Babylon is the only one of the Seven Wonders of the World that may not have actually existed.

☐   Historians and other researchers are still debating whether the gardens were real.

☐   They have been described in ancient texts, but no solid evidence has ever been found to prove that they were real.

☐   It is possible that they were an idea of a stunning and impressive garden and more of a legend than anything that was ever actually built.

☐   It is still part of the Seven Wonders because it is currently accepted that the gardens were real, but were destroyed.

☐   However, this conclusion is not supported by all experts.

5   Read this sentence from the passage.

They have been described in ancient texts, but no solid evidence has ever been found to prove that they were real.

As it is used in the sentence, what does the word *solid* mean?

Ⓐ   having three dimensions

Ⓑ   strongly built

Ⓒ   reliable or definite

Ⓓ   hard to the touch

6 Read these sentences from the passage.

> **The gardens were said to be 400 feet by 400 feet long. That is just over the size of three complete football fields.**

What is the main reason the author includes the second sentence above?

- Ⓐ to suggest one of the uses of the gardens
- Ⓑ to show the challenges created by the gardens
- Ⓒ to help readers imagine the size of the gardens
- Ⓓ to emphasize how much people enjoyed the gardens

7 Which of these would the author be best to include to help readers easily compare the locations of Babylon and Nineveh?

- Ⓐ graph
- Ⓑ map
- Ⓒ table
- Ⓓ timeline

8 Describe **two** ways the Great Pyramid of Giza is different from the Hanging Gardens of Babylon.

1: _____

_____

2: _____

_____

9   Use the information in paragraph 3 to complete the web below with **four** things that were found in the gardens other than plants.

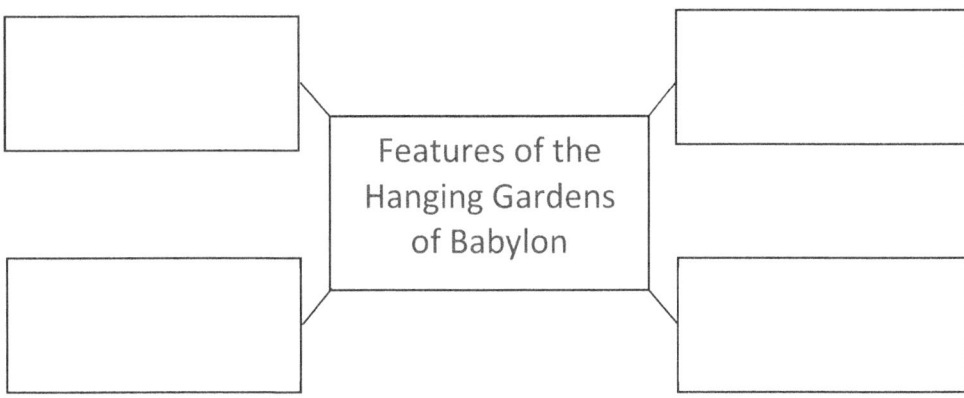

10 According to the theory described in the passage, why did King Nebuchadnezzar II build the gardens? Use **two** details from the passage to support your answer.

_____

_____

_____

_____

_____

11   Read this sentence from the passage.

> **A real garden that was quite impressive could have become a story about a wondrous structure.**

How does this sentence show the exaggeration that could have been involved in creating the myth of the Hanging Gardens of Babylon? Explain your answer.

_____

_____

_____

_____

_____

12   Describe **two** reasons that watering the gardens would have been difficult.

1: _____

_____

2: _____

_____

13. Some people argue that if the gardens were real, the remains of them would have been found. How does the information in the section titled "Where's the Evidence?" argue against this point? Explain your answer.

14. Do you think it will ever be proven that the Hanging Gardens of Babylon did really exist? Explain why you feel that way.

15 The passage describes three different theories on who created the Hanging Gardens. Summarize the three different theories. Use details from the passage to support your answer.

Practice Set 18

Speech

Women of the World

Instructions

This set has one passage for you to read. The passage is followed by questions.

Read each question carefully. For each multiple choice question, fill in the circle for the correct answer. For other types of questions, follow the instructions given. Some of the questions require a written answer. Write your answer on the lines provided.

Women of the World
Adapted from a Speech to the United Nations by Hillary Clinton

Fifteen years ago, delegates from 189 countries met in Beijing for the Fourth World Conference on Women. It was a call to action – a call to the global community to work for the laws, reforms, and social changes necessary to ensure that women and girls everywhere finally have the opportunities they deserve to fulfill their potential and contribute fully to society.

For many of us in this room today, that was a call to action that we have heeded. I know some of you have made it the cause of your life. You have worked tirelessly, day in and day out, to translate those words into realities. And we have seen the evidence of such great efforts everywhere.

In South Africa, women living in shanty towns came together to build a housing development outside Cape Town all on their own, brick by brick. And today, their community has grown to more than 50,000 homes for low income families, most of them female-headed.

In Liberia, a group of church women began a prayer movement to stop their country's brutal civil war. It grew to include thousands of women who helped force the two sides to negotiate a peace agreement. And then, those women helped elect Ellen Johnson Sirleaf president, the first woman to lead an African nation.

In the United States, a young woman had an idea for a website where anyone could help a small business on the other side of the world get off the ground. And today, the organization she co-founded, Kiva, has given more than $120 million in small loans to entrepreneurs in developing countries, 80 percent of them women.

So as we meet here in New York, women worldwide are working hard to do their part to improve the status of women and girls. And in so doing, they are also improving the status of families, communities, and countries. They are literally leaving their marks on the world. For example, thanks to the environmental movement started by Wangari Maathai, 45 million trees are now standing tall across Kenya. Maathai inspired thousands of women to plant trees in their regions.

Now, these are just a few of the stories, and everyone here could stand up and tell even more. These are the stories of what women around the world do every day to solve problems, propel economies, improve living conditions, and promote peace. Women have shown time and again that they will seize opportunities to improve their own and their families' lives. And even when it seems that no opportunity exists, they still find a way. And thanks to the hard work and persistence of women and men, we have made real gains.

But the progress we have made in the past 15 years is by no means the end of the story. There is still so much more to be done. We have to write the next chapter to fully realize the dreams and potential that we set forth in Beijing. Because for too many millions and millions of girls and women, opportunity remains out of reach.

Change on a global scale cannot and does not happen overnight. It takes time, patience, and persistence. And as hard as we have worked these past 15 years, we have more work to do. So today, let us renew our commitment to finishing the job. And let us intensify our efforts. It is both the right thing to do and it is the smart thing as well.

So whether we live in New York or New Delhi, Lagos or La Paz, women and girls share many of the same struggles and aspirations. The principle of women's equality is a simple truth, but the work of turning that principle into practice is rarely simple. It takes years and even generations of patient, persistent work, not only to change a country's laws, but to change its people's minds.

So we must measure our progress not by what we say in great venues like this, but in how well we are able to improve the condition of women's lives, some near at hand who deserve the opportunities many of us take for granted, some in far distant cities and remote villages – women we are not likely ever to meet but whose lives will be shaped by our actions.

Let us recommit ourselves, as individuals, as nations, as the United Nations, to build upon the progress of the past and achieve once and for all that principle that we all believe in, or we would not be here today. The rights and opportunities of all women and girls deserve our attention and our support because as they make progress, then the progress that should be the birthright of future generations will be more likely, and the 21st century will fulfill the promise that we hold out today. So let's go forth and be reenergized in the work that lies ahead.

1 In the first paragraph, Clinton refers to the Fourth World Conference on Women as "a call to action." This refers to a need to –

- Ⓐ meet again
- Ⓑ make changes
- Ⓒ speak to more women
- Ⓓ take more chances

2 How is the information in paragraph 4 of the speech organized?

- Ⓐ fact and opinion
- Ⓑ problem and solution
- Ⓒ compare and contrast
- Ⓓ chronological order

3 In the speech, what are the examples in paragraphs 3, 4, and 5 used to show?

- Ⓐ the problems that need to be solved
- Ⓑ the difference that women are making
- Ⓒ the changes that need to occur
- Ⓓ the reasons that improvements take time

4   Read this sentence from paragraph 6.

> **They are literally leaving their marks on the world.**

What does this sentence mean?

- Ⓐ   They are risking their lives.
- Ⓑ   They are sharing their stories.
- Ⓒ   They are making a difference.
- Ⓓ   They are supporting each other.

5   What do Clinton's words in paragraph 7 suggest about how she feels about women?

- Ⓐ   She respects and admires them.
- Ⓑ   She is concerned for them.
- Ⓒ   She is excited for them.
- Ⓓ   She doubts and mistrusts them.

6   Which phrase from paragraph 12 does Clinton use to emphasize the difference the United Nations can make to the lives of women? Select the **one** best answer.

- ☐   "we must measure our progress"
- ☐   "not by what we say in great venues like this"
- ☐   "deserve the opportunities many of us take for granted"
- ☐   "in far distant cities and remote villages"
- ☐   "women we are not likely ever to meet"
- ☐   "whose lives will be shaped by our actions"

7 In paragraph 2, Clinton highlights the effort people have put in. Underline **two** phrases from the paragraph that emphasize people's hard work.

> For many of us in this room today, that was a call to action that we have heeded. I know some of you have made it the cause of your life. You have worked tirelessly, day in and day out, to translate those words into realities. And we have seen the evidence of such great efforts everywhere.

8 Read this sentence from paragraph 3.

> **In South Africa, women living in shanty towns came together to build a housing development outside Cape Town all on their own, brick by brick.**

What do the words "brick by brick" suggest about the work the women did? Explain your answer.

_____

_____

_____

_____

9. How does the organization Kiva help women around the world help themselves and improve their own lives? Use **two** details from the passage to support your answer.

_____
_____
_____
_____
_____

10. The speech refers to the environmental movement started by Wangari Maathai. List **two** details Clinton uses to show that the actions she inspired were impressive.

1: _____
_____

2: _____
_____

11. In paragraph 7, how does Clinton show that women are determined? Use **two** details from the paragraph in your answer.

_____
_____
_____
_____
_____

12 How does Clinton's message to the audience change in paragraph 8? Explain.

_____

_____

_____

_____

_____

13 In which **two** sentences from paragraph 9 is Clinton stating to the audience what she wants them to agree to do? Select the **two** correct answers.

- ☐ Change on a global scale cannot and does not happen overnight.
- ☐ It takes time, patience, and persistence.
- ☐ And as hard as we have worked these past 15 years, we have more work to do.
- ☐ So today, let us renew our commitment to finishing the job.
- ☐ And let us intensify our efforts.
- ☐ It is both the right thing to do and it is the smart thing as well.

14 How do you think Clinton wants listeners to feel in the last paragraph? Explain.

_____

_____

_____

_____

_____

15. How does Clinton help listeners understand and respect what women can achieve? Use **three** examples from the speech of women's achievements to support your answer.

Answer Key

Our Solar System

Question	Answer
1	B
2	D
3	Dwarf planets: Ceres, Eris, Makemake, Haumea Moons: Io, Titan, Europa Asteroids: Ida, Gaspra
4	A
5	D
6	Mars: looks red Jupiter: giant red oval spot Saturn: has rings
7	A
8	B
9	The student should describe how the Sun tries to pull each planet toward it, and how each planet tries to pull away from the Sun. The student should explain that the forces balance each other and keep each planet in its orbit.
10	The student should complete the table with the data below. Distance for Mercury: 36 million miles Distance for Earth: 93 million miles Orbit time for Mercury: 88 days Orbit time for Earth: 365 days
11	The student should explain that the carbon dioxide makes the planet hot. The answer should refer to how the carbon dioxide traps heat from the Sun.
12	The student should give a reasonable explanation of how the section shows that understanding is always changing. The answer should refer to how Pluto was once considered a planet, but is now known as a dwarf planet.
13	The student should list how Io has active volcanoes and how Titan has lakes, rivers, and oceans.
14	The student should relate the art to how scientists learn about the Solar System. The student may refer to space exploration, to the use of robots and rovers, to taking photographs, to collecting data, or to using tools to study the Solar System.
15	The student should give a reasonable comparison of the four gas planets and use relevant supporting details from the passage. The answer may refer to their locations, their sizes, their physical features, their moons, or what they are made of.

Louis Braille – Inventor of Braille for the Blind

Question	Answer
1	B
2	C
3	D
4	Night Writing – ticks for 1st, 2nd, 4th, and 5th Braille – ticks for 1st, 3rd, 4th, and 6th
5	A
6	1852
7	B
8	The student should describe how a cell is a group of six dots, with three dots lined up in two rows. The student may include that a cell stands for a letter, punctuation mark, or symbol.
9	The student should describe how meeting Charles Barbier gave Louis the idea for Braille or the starting point for Braille. The student should describe how Louis changed and improved Barbier's night writing code to create Braille.
10	The student should describe how the sentences show how Braille is used by blind people in everyday life, how Braille helps blind people, or why Braille is important to people.
11	The student should give a reasonable description of what the word "gift" suggests about how people feel about Braille. The answer may refer to how people appreciate Braille or are glad it was created.
12	Similarities: They are both machines. / They have keys. / They are used to type. Differences: Typewriters have over 50 keys. / Braillewriters have only 6 keys. / Braillewriters have keys that stand for dots.
13	The student should list how people can use software programs to write and edit Braille and how people can carry small electronic devices around.
14	The student should refer to how both photographs show a person reading Braille by feeling the letters. The answer should refer to how Braille is read with the hands.
15	The student should describe three events in Louis's early life that led him to create Braille. The answer should refer to Louis becoming blind as a child, Louis being frustrated at school because he wanted to read, and Louis meeting Charles Barbier and being told about the night writing code.

Reading Skills Workbook, Focus on Nonfiction, Grade 5

Book Review: *Love That Dog*

Question	Answer
1	B
2	unique
3	The student should use two details from the first paragraph to explain why the book is unique. The answer may refer to how it is told using diary entries, how the diary entries include poems, or how it tells a story and explores how to understand and write poems.
4	A
5	B
6	D
7	C
8	The student should explain that Jack starts writing poetry because his teacher gives him an assignment to and that Jack copies other poems because he does not know how to write poetry.
9	The student should explain that the author has Jack mentioning a blue car and shows that it is important but does not explain why. The student should explain how making the reader wonder about this creates suspense.
10	The student may list how the author started writing poetry of her own, enjoyed reading the poems that Jack referenced in the book, learned about poetry by reading Jack's diary entries, or learned how to take poems and change them to create your own version.
11	The student should explain that "have readers in stitches" refers to making readers laugh and that "find yourself hooked" refers to being very interested or being unable to stop reading.
12	The student should explain that the technique described is taking someone else's poem and changing the words to make it about something else.
13	The student should explain that the author is worried that the book will not seem exciting or entertaining enough and is not the type of book that many students choose to read. The answer may refer to how the author compares it to other types of books or refers to readers thinking that it sounds boring.
14	The student should describe how the two poems show how Jack took a famous poem about a red wheelbarrow and changed the words so it was about his dog Sky being hit by a blue car. The student should describe how the poems show how Jack changes poems to tell his story.
15	The student should describe what makes *Love That Dog* unique and original and include at least three supporting details from the passage. The answer may refer to its unique structure, how it uses poetry to tell a story, or to how it is both a story and a book that helps readers understand and write poems.

Reading Skills Workbook, Focus on Nonfiction, Grade 5

Ready to Roll

Question	Answer
1	D
2	C
3	Step 4
4	The student may list how fillings are placed between items or how it can be made with any fillings you choose. The student may also list their own ideas, such as it being easy to make, being made with your hands, or being a good snack or lunch idea.
5	2. Sheet of nori 6. Sharp knife The student should give a reasonable explanation of why a list of items would be helpful. The answer could refer to helping someone making sushi be organized or allowing someone making sushi to collect everything they need.
6	The student should relate the art of the perfect sushi rolls and the caption to the information in steps 6 through 8. The answer may refer to how the sushi has to be rolled neatly, pressed firmly enough to hold everything together, pressed so that all the rolls will be the same shape and will not be squashed, or cut carefully.

Get Planting!

Question	Answer
1	C
2	C
3	Step 7
4	The student should explain that the sentences support the idea that trees get enough water from natural rainfall and do not need to be watered all the time.
5	1: Choose a tree that is <u>suited to your climate</u>. 2: Place the tree where it will get enough <u>sunlight</u> and <u>rain/water</u>.
6	The student should give a reasonable explanation of how the instructions support the idea that growing a tree "only takes a little bit of effort in the beginning." The answer may describe planting a tree as only requiring a few simple steps, may refer to all the steps as being done at the beginning, or may describe how the only things to do after the plants starts to grow is to wait for it to grow.

Bike Hire

Question	Answer
1	D
2	B
3	The student should list that the bikes are better for the environment and that there will be less traffic.
4	The student should give an opinion on whether the author makes a convincing argument and provide reasonable support for the opinion. The answer may refer to the comparison to the cost of a taxi and a bus, the benefits of bike hire over using the bus, or the savings of being able to borrow a bike instead of buying one.
5	The student should identify that Step 1 supports the idea. The answer should refer to how the map in the step shows that there are bikes at several different locations.
6	The student should explain that the checks would be best to be done at Step 2 when picking a bike. The answer may describe how these are things to check when choosing a suitable bike, or how it would be too late at Step 8 since the bike would have already been selected and paid for at this point.

Make the Most of Your Time: Give it to Others!

Question	Answer
1	The student should circle the phrase "everyone in our school."
2	C
3	C
4	A
5	The web should be completed with any three of the actions below. by planting trees, by picking up litter, by removing graffiti, by repainting park benches
6	"everyone followed my instructions"
7	D
8	C
9	The student should explain that Carly does not mind that it was hard work because it was worth it. The answer may refer to how she says she felt amazing, how the people were grateful, or how pleased the people were.
10	The student should explain that Carly was thrilled to hear of the project involving painting the murals because of her interest in art. The answer may refer to how she knew she could use her skills to help, how art is one of her passions, or how she played a big role in the project.
11	The student should explain that Carly was surprised that the other volunteers did not mind her young age and accepted her. The answer may refer to how the older people accepted her as a leader during the mural project or how she worried that "nobody would want a kid around to help."
12	The student may list how volunteering helps you learn to work with people of all backgrounds, helps you learn to communicate, helps you learn to work as part of a team, helps you learn how to be a leader, or is something you could put on a college application.
13	The student should give a reasonable explanation of why Carly asks questions. The student may describe how the questions challenge students, ask students to think about their choices, or encourage students to view how they use their spare time differently.
14	The student should explain that Carly considers helping others as being a wise use of time. The answer may refer to Carly telling people not to waste time on meaningless tasks and to spend time doing something important and something that helps others.
15	The student should describe how Carly uses her own experiences to make readers feel positive and excited about volunteering and use relevant supporting details. The answer may refer to how Carly feels about helping others, the benefits she gets from volunteering, or how she has been able to use her own skills.

Robotics Classes

Question	Answer
1	D
2	D
3	B
4	B
5	The student should explain that the author compares students who feel confident about learning robotics with students who feel unsure or feel it will be too difficult. The answer should describe how this comparison supports the idea that the classes will be tailored to each student's needs.
6	The student should list how parents want their children to learn new things, have a wide range of interests, be engaged in after-school activities, and how parents want to be involved in the child's learning.
7	B
8	B
9	The student should describe how the author creates enthusiasm in the first paragraph. The answer could refer to the questions asked, to the positive description of the classes, to the mention of bringing things to life, to referring to the classes as an "amazing opportunity," or to describing how people will be able to build robots to wow family and friends.
10	The student should list how teachers do not need to understand robotics and how all the equipment needed is provided.
11	The student should describe how it could be a family activity because parents can also be involved and attend the classes. The answer should refer to how parents are welcome to join in and how parents can also build robots.
12	The student should give a reasonable explanation of how the classes solve the problem of teachers feeling nervous about teaching robotics. The answer may describe how teachers do not have to teach the subject, how the robotics kits are easy to use, how skilled instructors provide guidance, or how teachers can join the class.
13	The student should identify that students are not able to organize robotics classes. The answer should show an understanding that students can tell their parents and teachers about the classes, but that the schools will need to actually organize and book the classes.
14	Go to the website and request a visit from a sales team. → Attend a demonstration of the classes. → Discuss the classes with the sales team. → Visit the website and complete an order online.
15	The student should give a summary of how the robotics classes benefit students, parents, and schools. The answer should use relevant supporting details from the passage.

How to Make Magical Rice Krispie Treats

Question	Answer
1	A
2	D
3	C
4	A
5	Step 7, Step 10, Step 13
6	C
7	yummy treats, fun games, clown, magician
8	The student may list how the area should be clean, how there should be plenty of free space, how everyone should have washed their hands, how all the ingredients should be measured out, or how all the magical ingredients should be laid out ready.
9	The student should explain that the gloves need to be worn to stop your hands from getting dirty or messy. The answer may refer to the steps involving touching ingredients or the step where you spray your hands with cooking spray.
10	The student should explain that the cooking spray is used to grease your hands so the mixture does not stick to your hands when you are forming it into balls.
11	The student should give a reasonable similarity and difference between the two steps. The answer may refer to how both steps involve adding the magical ingredients, but how Step 7 mixes it in while Step 10 has the ingredients sprinkled on top.
12	The student should list the size as being about the size of a ping pong ball and the shape as being a small ball.
13	The student should give a reasonable explanation of how each Rice Krispie Treat is colorful. The answer may refer to adding food coloring or to adding the colorful magical ingredients like gold sugar, rainbow sprinkles, or colored caramel drizzle.
14	The student should relate the photograph to the description of putting the treats on sticks and using them as table decorations.
15	The student should describe three ways that Magical Rice Krispie Treats could be made unique. The answer could refer to the colors used, the range of magical ingredients used, using different magical ingredients, dipping the treats in chocolate, forming them in different shapes, placing them on sticks, or any other reasonable answer.

Climate Change – What Can You Do?

Question	Answer
1	B
2	C
3	D
4	D
5	turning off lights, unplugging computers, washing dishes by hand, using energy saving light globes
6	Cars produce greenhouse gas emissions, but bicycles do not and walking certainly does not.
7	C
8	B
9	The student should explain that a fridge uses a lot of energy and is on all the time.
10	The student should give a reasonable explanation of how people need to find a balance. The answer should relate to being comfortable, but also using heating and cooling responsibly. The answer could refer to setting the thermostat lower and wearing a sweater or using a fan instead of central cooling.
11	The student should list using cold water to wash clothes and hanging your clothes up to dry instead of using an electric dryer.
12	The student should explain that recycling paper and cardboard means that fewer trees need to be cut down and should also explain that trees reduce greenhouse gases.
13	The student should identify that the photograph of the tires is an example of reusing things. The answer may refer to how old tires have been reused to make plant pots or borders for gardens.
14	The student should list how people can buy food that is grown locally and can grow their own vegetables.
15	The student should give an opinion on whether or not the author does a good job of convincing readers to change. The student could argue that the author does a good job and explain what the author has done well. This could refer to showing what the problem is, giving simple examples of actions to take, being encouraging, or suggesting that everyone can make a difference. The student could also argue that the author does not do a good job and tell how the author could do a better job. This could refer to making the problem seem more serious, making readers care more about the topic, or being more demanding.

Journey to the Deep Ocean

Question	Answer
1	B
2	Guam, Pacific Ocean, 36,000 feet
3	A
4	B
5	It was made super strong. It was fitted with oxygen systems. It had lights fitted to the inside and outside.
6	4th and 5th
7	B
8	C
9	The student should list how James wanted to explore and see what was down there and how James wanted to collect data for scientific analysis.
10	The student should relate the quote about curiosity to James Cameron's interest in exploring the deep ocean. The answer may describe how the quote shows how powerful curiosity is and how James was curious enough about the deep ocean to organize a journey to explore the area.
11	The student may infer that James is surprised, shocked, annoyed, or puzzled that more is known about Mars than the deep ocean. The student should use supporting details to explain the inference, such as how James wondered why it was so and asked himself why people had not explored it.
12	The student should explain that there was a fluid leak that made it hard to see and drive the submarine and that there were faults that made it hard to collect samples.
13	The student should explain that having butterflies in your stomach refers to feeling nervous. The student should describe how the sentence shows how James felt.
14	The student may list how James had faith in the quality of the vessel, felt the vessel had been designed and built well, or how he felt confident the vessel would do the job.
15	The student should describe two disappointments of the journey and use relevant supporting details from the passage. The answer may refer to how James was not able to explore the ocean floor for as long as he hoped to, how he was not able to see or drive the submarine easily, how it was hard to collect samples, or how he only saw small shrimplike creatures and did not see as many living things as he expected.

Reading Skills Workbook, Focus on Nonfiction, Grade 5

The First Moon Landing

Question	Answer
1	A
2	D
3	B
4	B
5	D
6	The student should select the boxes described below. Neil Armstrong – all 3; Buzz Aldrin – first two; Michael Collins – first
7	The student should circle the phrases "more impressive to mankind" and "more important for the long-range exploration of space."
8	The student should explain that the missions before Apollo 11 show that it required years of preparation to be ready for the Moon landing. The answer may refer to how all the missions were needed for Apollo 11 to succeed.
9	The student should describe *Eagle* as the lunar module and refer to how it traveled to the surface of the Moon. The student should describe *Columbia* as the control module and refer to how it stayed in orbit around the Moon.
10	The student should complete the web with the actions listed below. collected samples, took photos, put up a flag
11	The student should give a reasonable explanation as to why Collins would be thrilled. The student may infer that he would have been worried about Armstrong and Aldrin or hoping that the mission would be successful.
12	The student should explain that the flag would not have flown on the Moon because there is no wind there and that the wire was put in to make it look like it was flying. The student may infer that they wanted the flag to look like a positive symbol and not to be flopped down sadly.
13	The student should complete the three missing entries as shown below. July 19 – Apollo 11 began orbiting the Moon July 20, 3:17 p.m. – the *Eagle* landed on the Moon July 20, 9:56 p.m. – Armstrong stepped onto the Moon
14	The student may list how more astronauts would make the journey, how ten more people reached the Moon's surface, how it was a great achievement for scientists and engineers, or how it paved the way for future space exploration.
15	The student should give a reasonable explanation of how the first Moon landing is something Americans should be proud of and use relevant supporting details. The answer may refer to how great an achievement it was, how much preparation and planning it took, how many people worked together to make it possible, or how it amazed and inspired people.

Reading Skills Workbook, Focus on Nonfiction, Grade 5

Tennis Camp

Question	Answer
1	B
2	D
3	D
4	A
5	The student should list two details that support the idea that the tennis camp's main purpose is to make good players better. The answer could refer to the daily training drills, the trainers who are professional tennis players, or the contest at the end of the camp.
6	The student should describe how the author supports the idea that students will learn from the best. The answer may refer to how all the trainers are professional tennis players, how some trainers have won major tournaments, or how one of the trainers is one of America's top ten junior players.

Cameron's Photography Courses

Question	Answer
1	B
2	C
3	The student should give a reasonable explanation of the meaning of the statement. The answer should refer to how a camera allows you to capture anything you like, and should refer to how Cameron wants students to be excited about what they could photograph.
4	The student should list how Cameron has been a professional photographer for 15 years, has been published all around the world, has won many awards, or is famous for taking photographs of birds and other wildlife.
5	The student should relate the illustration of the photographer to Cameron being a photographer of birds and wildlife. The answer may refer to how he looks like he is dressed for outdoors, or may specifically refer to his backpack and his facial hair as suggesting someone who spends time outdoors.
6	The student should state an opinion on whether the flyer makes the courses seem serious or fun and support it with relevant details from the flyer. The student could refer to specific details like all the equipment shown or the smiling photographer, or could be general and refer to the cartoonish art.

Reading Skills Workbook, Focus on Nonfiction, Grade 5

The Circus is Coming to Town

Question	Answer
1	D
2	Get Your Tickets Now
3	A
4	The student should state that either the acrobats, clowns, exotic animals, or Hercules Man would most amaze people. The student should include a reasonable explanation to support the opinion.
5	The student should identify the detail about it being the 13th annual festival as showing that the circus has been held many times before. The student should refer to how it has been held every year for 13 years.
6	The student should give a reasonable description of how two specific examples of art make the circus seem fun and exciting. The answer could refer to the fireworks, the tent, the way the word "circus" has lights, the seal, or the stars around the border.

Farm Fresh Tomato Sauce

Question	Answer
1	D
2	A
3	The student may list the whole tomatoes next to the bottle, the tomatoes on the vines, or the farm in the background.
4	The student should complete the table by listing how the family has been making tomato sauce for generations and how the advertisement describes the product as being around since 1880.
5	The student should list two differences between the tomato sauce and the other products listed. The student may list how it has more uses, is a simpler product, does not contain anything other than tomato, is the first product, or is the best-selling product.
6	The student should give an opinion on whether the art would help sell the product. The student may argue either way as long as the opinion is supported with a reasonable explanation.

Durian Food Products

Question	Answer
1	A
2	The student should list how durians are banned on Singapore subways and how a plane was delayed because passengers could smell a crate of durians.
3	Durian Yogurt Durian Jelly Spread Durian Juice
4	The student should describe how the advertisement shows six different products of different types and uses. The answer should describe how the products show the wide variety of products available.
5	The student should give a reasonable explanation of how the products make it easier for people to try durian. The answer may refer to how the company has turned the tricky fruit into usable products, has made subtle and balanced products, has made products that are ready to eat, or have used the strange fruit in products that people are used to eating.
6	The student should give an opinion on whether or not the passage created curiosity about trying the fruit. Students could describe how the details about the uniqueness made them want to try it, or how the details about the strong smell and strange taste made them not want to try it.

Summer Crush Smoothies

Question	Answer
1	A
2	D
3	The student should explain that seasonal means only for a season or containing fruit from the current season and that limited means only for a certain time.
4	The student should give a reasonable similarity and difference. The similarity could be that they both contain panna cotta, both contain summer fruit, or that they look similar. The difference should be that one contains kiwifruit and the other contains strawberries and blueberries.
5	The student may list the phrase "cool and refreshing," the phrases "beat the heat" or "ice-cold treat," or the illustration of the sun.
6	The student should give a personal opinion on whether "Summer Crush" is a good name for the products. The opinion should be supported and explained.

Reading Skills Workbook, Focus on Nonfiction, Grade 5

Exploring the Deep

Question	Answer
1	B
2	B
3	3rd and 5th
4	A
5	C
6	The student should list any four of the words below. incredible, unique, strange, weird, alien-like
7	C
8	The student should describe how the author uses examples of some deep ocean creatures. The answer may refer to the giant tube worms, the Dumbo octopus, or creatures that glow.
9	The student should describe how scientists are able to control D2 and see everything that the robot's camera sees. The answer may refer to how explorers cannot travel to the deep ocean, but can send robots like D2 to explore it.
10	The student should list how they thought the pressure would be too great and how they thought animals could not survive without sunlight.
11	The student should list any three of the following physical features. big ears/big floppy ears, 12 inches long, big eyes, spreads out its tentacles
12	The student should list how it has big floppy ears and how it is able to survive thousands of feet below sea level.
13	The student should underline or highlight the phrase "shoot light out into the water like fireworks." The student may describe how it helps readers imagine the light shooting out, imagine the brightness of the light, or imagine the movement of the light.
14	The student should show an understanding that scuba divers can explore shallow water but could not explore the deep ocean. The answer should refer to how the pressure would be too great.
15	The student should give a reasonable explanation of how scientists would have felt and use relevant supporting details from the passage. The student may describe scientists as being shocked, surprised, puzzled, or excited by the finds. The answer may refer to how scientists did not think life could survive in the deep ocean, or may refer to the unusual animals found.

Babe Ruth

Question	Answer
1	C
2	A
3	D
4	D
5	C
6	C
7	B
8	The student may list how Matthias was a role model, how Matthias taught Babe about baseball, how Matthias helped develop Babe's baseball skills, or how Matthias helped Babe develop a love for baseball.
9	The student may list pitching 13 scoreless innings in one game, hitting 11 home runs in 1918, or hitting 29 home runs in 1919.
10	The student should describe how the Boston Red Sox had financial problems and sold Babe for $100,000 to raise money.
11	The student may refer to how Babe was a superstar, how people came to watch Babe play, or how people wanted to see Babe's talent for themselves.
12	The table should be completed with the details below. 1918 – 11, 1919 – 29, 1920 – 54, 1921 – 59, 1927 – 60
13	The student should describe how Babe Ruth's number of home runs increased over time and identify that this shows that he improved over time.
14	The student may list how he helped charities, how he had his own charity called the Babe Ruth Foundation, or how he left much of his money to the Babe Ruth Foundation.
15	The student should write an essay supporting the idea that Babe Ruth's achievements have not been forgotten. The student may include details about how he set records, how he has statues in his honor, how he was added to the Baseball Hall of Fame, how he is still known as one of the greatest baseball players of all time, or how young baseball players today still admire him.

Reading Skills Workbook, Focus on Nonfiction, Grade 5

How to Write a Short Story

Question	Answer
1	B
2	A
3	B
4	C
5	B
6	Brainstorming – generating ideas Making an Outline – planning writing Starting to Write – creating writing Revising and Editing Process – improving writing
7	B
8	The student should give a reasonable explanation of how a writer is like an inventor. The answer should refer to how the author describes writers as creating a whole new world and how they can create anything they can imagine.
9	The student may list how it is a way for people to express themselves, that it is a way of being creative, how it is suitable for people of all ages, or how it is a hobby that does not need special equipment.
10	The student should describe how freewriting helps writers start thinking and come up with new ideas, and explain that this could be a way of brainstorming.
11	The student should explain that the photograph shows the problems that can occur if you do not have an outline. The answer should refer to how the boy looks frustrated or annoyed or how he seems to be having trouble writing.
12	The student may list fixing things that don't make sense, adding important information that may have been forgotten, fixing writing that repeats itself, fixing grammar errors, or improving sentence structure.
13	The student should describe the benefits of having someone else read the story. The answer may refer to getting honest feedback, to someone else being able to see what works and what doesn't, or to someone else having new ideas that you may not have thought of.
14	The student may list how the author describes how writing improves with practice, how the author relates great and famous writers as having practiced, or how the author suggests that people use a journal to write every day.
15	The student should give a reasonable explanation of why creating an outline is an important step and use relevant details from the passage. The answer may refer to the outline as helping an idea turn into a story, as helping a writer stay focused and organized, as helping writers know where to start, or as being a guide to what the whole story needs to contain.

Children and Cell Phones

Question	Answer
1	D
2	A
3	C
4	D
5	B
6	D
7	A
8	The student should explain how the statement describes how children are using technology instead of playing sports or doing physical activities.
9	The student should list how the author describes how her 4 year old daughter doesn't know how to play hopscotch and how many kids do not know what hide-and-go-seek is.
10	The student should describe how sleep is easy and restful for people who have played outside, while people using their phones all day find it hard to sleep.
11	The student should describe the example of young people watching their older siblings play games on their phones and describe how young people want to copy this behavior.
12	The student should list how young people do not learn how to make friends and have difficulty talking to people their own age.
13	The student should identify that the author wants parents, teachers, coaches, and other role models to read the letter and think about what they can do to help solve the problem.
14	The student should describe how children playing outdoors feel relaxed, happy, joyful, or positive about spending time with others. The student may compare this to how people feel when playing on their phones.
15	The student should give an opinion on whether or not he or she agrees that children having cell phones is a serious problem. Either answer is acceptable as long as it is supported with a reasonable explanation. The student may use details from the passage, their own ideas, or their own examples or personal experiences to support the opinion.

The Hanging Gardens of Babylon

Question	Answer
1	A
2	D
3	C
4	Historians and other researchers are still debating whether the gardens were real. However, this conclusion is not supported by all experts.
5	C
6	C
7	B
8	The student may list that the Great Pyramid of Giza is still standing today, definitely existed, or is much older.
9	The student should complete the web with the features listed below. waterfalls, exotic creatures, vaults, arches
10	The student should explain that the king built the gardens to make his wife happy because she missed the greenery of her homeland.
11	The student should describe how the sentence tells how people could have exaggerated to make a garden seem much greater than it really was. The student should describe how this explains how the myth of the gardens could have been created.
12	The student should list how the gardens were massive and would have required a lot of water and how the gardens were tall and would have required the water to be transported to the top.
13	The student should describe how the information in "Where's the Evidence?" shows that the remains of the garden could still be hidden under the Euphrates River and just may not have been found yet.
14	The student should give an opinion on whether he or she feels that the gardens will ever be proven to exist. The student may argue either way but the answer should be supported with a reasonable explanation.
15	The student should summarize the three theories on who created the Hanging Gardens of Babylon and use relevant supporting details. The answer should summarize the theories that King Nebuchadnezzar II built them for this wife, that Queen Semiramis built them as one of her building projects, and that King Sennacherib had impressive gardens in Nineveh that became confused with the gardens of Babylon.

Women of the World

Question	Answer
1	B
2	D
3	B
4	C
5	A
6	"whose lives will be shaped by our actions"
7	The student could underline any of the phrases listed below. cause of your life, worked tirelessly, day in and day out, such great efforts
8	The student should give a reasonable explanation of what the words "brick by brick" suggest. The answer may refer to it suggesting that the women worked hard, worked for a long time, were patient, or did it one small step at a time.
9	The student should explain that Kiva allows women to borrow money to start their own businesses. The student should relate getting these loans to taking action to improve one's own life by starting a business.
10	The student should list how 45 million trees have been planted across Kenya and how thousands of women have been inspired to plant trees.
11	The student should explain how Clinton shows that women are determined. The answer should refer to how Clinton refers to women as seizing opportunities to improve their lives and finding a way even when it seems that no opportunity exists.
12	The student should describe how the speech changes in paragraph 8. The answer could refer to the speech as now looking forward instead of to the past, looking at what more needs to be done instead of what has already been done, or becoming less positive and more focused on how change is still needed.
13	4th and 5th
14	The student should give a reasonable opinion on how Clinton wants listeners to feel in the last paragraph. The student may infer that Clinton wants listeners to feel positive, hopeful, determined, or motivated.
15	The student should explain how Clinton helps listeners understand and respect what women can achieve and support the answer by giving three examples of achievements. The examples given could include women in Cape Town building a housing development, women in Liberia beginning a prayer movement, an American woman starting Kiva, or Wangari Maathai starting an environmental movement.

Made in the USA
Middletown, DE
09 April 2025

74053406R00113